Message to Love

The Isle of Wight Festivals, 1968–70

Photographs: The Cameron Life Collection

Printed by: Staples Printers Rochester Limited,
Neptune Close, Medway City Estate, Frindsbury, Rochester, Kent.

Copyright: Brian Hinton, 1995.

Published by Castle Communications plc, A29 Barwell Business Park,
Leatherhead Road, Chessington, Surrey KT9 2NY.

ISBN: 1-86074-147-9

Message to Love

The Isle of Wight Festivals, 1968–70

by
Brian Hinton

Dedication

For Iain Sinclair

I'd never walked so far. I used to hitch: Aldermaston, Beaulieu Jazz Festival, Horovitz and Brown, the Isle of Wight. But no more.

Radon Daughters (1994), Chapter 14
From the Tape Diaries of Dr T.C.P. Hinton

Contents

Introduction

The great pop festivals of the late 1960s were very much a product of their times – youthful rebellion, music as popular art, a derangement of all the senses – but their underlying search for shared freedom and community had deep cultural roots. They contained within themselves the notions of a religious coming together, of a grown up boy-scouts camp making do in the open air – of a bohemian escape to a land of free love and illegal substances, of a waking dream, even of medieval pilgrimage.

Journeying to the Isle of Wight was itself part of the experience, so that queueing for the ferry, the crossing of water – and the proximity of the sea to all three sites – even the long trek to the site itself, all became an unforgettable adventure. Even the discomforts were special; the long queues for an overpriced hamburger or an overcrowded loo, or the struggle to get a good vantage point all made the music and sense of togetherness more worthwhile.

The three Island festivals were part of a wider experience. During the heyday of the Beatles, pop concerts were still (often) ill-assorted packages of twenty-minute sets. Dylan was one of the few performers who could be relied on to carry a whole evening by himself – and that was seen as 'folk music'. When Pink Floyd booked the Queen Elizabeth Hall for their Games For May concert in early 1967, it was the first time a 'pop' group had dared to be so unreasonable.

And yet this was the beginning of a new phase in rock music. Albums were becoming more than a few hit singles and lots of filler. Groups were beginning to stretch out from three-minute hits to long and involved improvisations. The Floyd, and the English underground scene at clubs like Middle Earth and UFO were responding in a typically English, quirky way to what was happening in San Francisco, where dances were mutating into concert happenings, and groups like the Grateful Dead were playing, literally, for hours.

With a great leap forward in technology – multitrack studios, the advent of stereo, vastly more powerful sound and lighting systems (film of the Beatles at Shea stadium is laughable in the paucity of equipment on show, drowned out easily by screaming girls), pop was mutating into rock.

The Beatles themselves had led the way, rescuing rock 'n' roll – white boys with loud guitars – from a morass of Tin Pan Alley rubbish, and gradually moving from covers of hardcore R&B to completely writing their own material.

In turn, Bob Dylan had made rock lyrics literate, even if completely incomprehensible as, in a series of cataclysmic concerts with the Hawks – later the Band – he rampaged around the known world, inventing the term folk–rock as he went, and drawing acclaim and vicious abuse in equal measure.

Meanwhile a handful of weird-beards, dope fiends and washed-up Beats living in a fading Victorian suburb of San Francisco were putting into practice the crazy notion of making rock music the equivalent of spaced-out, electronic string quartets, music for the space age.

And in London, an ex R&B rhythm guitarist, part black, part American Indian, who played his instrument strung upside down – occasionally with his teeth – was reinventing the electric guitar as the 'voice' of this new improvisation. Jimi Hendrix made sheer musicianship a thing of wonder.

Suddenly, anything was possible. Rock had colonised all other, rigidly defined, kinds of music – pop, classical, folk, jazz – and turned them into something new and strange. Allied to all this was an explosion in visual awareness (fuelled by something stronger than brown ale), which took in concert posters, light shows and rainbow-coloured clothes. In fact the whole was becoming what would later be pinned down as a new 'lifestyle', with all that implied; media overkill, unfunny jokes by worn out comedians, rumours of sin and depravity.

For English teenagers, this seemed indeed a forbidden paradise, with Scott Mackenzie as a willing tour guide, and beads and bells – not to mention cut flowers – rapidly infiltrated London and beyond. Pirate radio stations and the rapidly burgeoning underground press soon began to cater to this new taste for the weird and the wonderful. Even the names of West Coast bands – The Mystery Trend, Wizards From Kansas, Peanut Butter Conspiracy, Mad River – were a revelation, like something hatched up on Mars.

All this was reflected, on our side of the Atlantic, in an innocent, humourous way which lacked (as yet) the dangerous overtones of the States. Here Vietnam was an issue, not an ever-present threat; long hair was met with disapproval, not a possible hail of bullets.

It was as a response to the already mythical Festival at Monterey in June 1967 – when the cream of the SF groups, as well as the Who and expatriate American Jimi Hendrix were for the first time competently 'marketed' – and to various pale imitations here at home, that the Isle of Wight Indoor Swimming Pool Association decided to sponsor a one-day event on the Bank Holiday Saturday of 31 August, 1968.

From little acorns...

Festival Log

1956–1968

1955–61
Beaulieu Jazz Festivals
Ended after last two erupt into violence as opposing camps of modern
and trad fans heckle each other's heroes.

August 1961
First National Jazz Festival
Richmond, Surrey

26 July, 1963
Newport Folk Festival
New discovery Bob Dylan sings 'Blowing In The Wind'.

26–27 July, 1965
Newport Folk Festival
Rhode Island, USA

Dylan horrifies folk purists by appearing with the Paul Butterfield Blues Band and playing an electric set; he is roundly booed for his presumption.

8 August, 1965
National Jazz And Blues Festival
Richmond, Surrey
The jazz is interspersed with wild young R&B acts like the Rolling Stones, Yardbirds and Manfred Mann.

16 October, 1965
A Tribute To Dr Strange
Longshoreman's Hall, SF

4 January, 1966
First Acid Test At The Fillmore
Haight Ashbury, SF

1 August, 1966
National Jazz And Blues Festival
Windsor, Berkshire
The Who establish themselves as the new bad boys of rock; their 'auto-destructive' art leads sections of the audience to smash chairs and rip up the tents. Organiser Howard Pendleton is accused of 'lowering morals'!

15 October, 1966
International Times Launch
Roundhouse, London
Soft Machine and Pink Floyd; Paul McCartney dresses up as an arab and Marianne Faithfull as a nun!

14 January, 1967
The First Human Be-In
Golden Gate Park, SF

Local bands and thousands of newly invented hippies gather to celebrate the Summer of Love early, with appearances by Quicksilver Messenger Service and the Grateful Dead.

29 April, 1967
24 Hour Technicolour Dream
Alexandra Palace, London
The coming together of the English underground.

5 June, 1967
The Fair In The Woods
Mount Tamalpais, California
The Airplane, Doors, Byrds and Country Joe. Everyone dresses in medieval costume and gets happy.

16–18 June, 1967
Monterey Pop Festival
California
The cream of the new West Coast sound – including Country Joe And The Fish, Big Brother, and Jefferson Airplane – with Otis Redding joining the Love generation shortly before his death. Jimi Hendrix and the Who top the bill. Organised by John Phillips of the Mamas And Papas. Brian Jones wanders, like a prince, through the subsequent film. The Festival lives on, years later, as a book and CD box set. Seven hours worth of sound tapes subsequently materialise, and are broadcast on Radio 1, in perfect stereo.

26–28 August, 1967
Festival Of The Flower Children
Woburn Abbey, UK
The British response, with mind-expanding combos like Marmalade and the Bee Gees. Free flowers and sparklers are provided, with a

firework display every night. Organised by the Duke of Bedford.

31 August, 1968

Great South Coast Bank Holiday Pop Festival
Godshill, Isle of Wight
First UK visit of Jefferson Airplane.

1

1968 – Monterey meets Middle Earth, near Godshill

In the words of the Move's road manager, after the group blew nine speakers during their performance on a stage made from two trailers covered by scaffolding and canvas, 'It's a great louse-up!' This was a little uncharitable. Despite the inspired amateur nature of the proceedings – a West Coast happening reborn as a boy-scout camp – the 'GREAT South Coast Bankholiday POP FESTIVITY' was a magical, mysterious affair which lives long in the memories of all those lucky enough to attend. The groups who played were in the vanguard, from both sides of the Atlantic, of the new music, and rough energy made up for occasionally dodgy technique. The spirit of psychedelia shone through, and the intimacy of the occasion was somewhat lost in the two massive festivals which were to follow.

Site manager Ron Smith remembers setting up the event.

'The IOW pop festivals came about as a result of the Isle of Wight Swimming Pool Association, of which I was a member, wanting to raise funds. It was suggested we employ a fund-raiser. I said I knew someone; that person was Ronnie Foulk. We then proposed, after some discussion with Ray, that we have a pop

festival. The committee allocated £750 and we set about putting a festival together.

'Rikki Farr was chosen as compere; I met him at my home in Totland and a couple of days later we went out to the Festival site, which we had managed to acquire from Jimmy Flux. It was Hells Field, a one hundred acre field of stubble corn, and we paced out with some broken bars that had been left on the site what we thought the arena should be, and then Ronnie and Rikki Farr suddenly said, "We're off to London now, see you. Don't forget, it goes on in three weeks time, Ron."

'I wondered what I should do, when three brothers aged about thirty came on the scene in a van and said they'd heard we were talking about a pop festival on the Island and could they help. They had called at my house and the missus had sent them out. They wanted desperately to be involved, and had experience in scaffolding, laying bricks, anything.

'So I went off in my van to get some scaffolding poles and we set to to build the stadium. We covered it with black plastic. The stage was several low loaders which I had through the good offices of British Road Services, and we got a generator down from Winchester. Water for the site was obtained in new dustbins by my wife, who went round garages in the area, filling them up.

'We started to build the site one week before the groups arrived. On the Friday night, two members of Jefferson Airplane arrived at my house, while I was having dinner, and we went to the site. The show went on the next morning, and the weather wasn't too bad; during the night it rained a bit but the kids didn't move. Everyone enjoyed it.

'One of the things that stuck in my mind was as follows. We had outside of the plastic and scaffolding fence a rope stretched on short posts about five yards away, giving a no-go area all round, patrolled by local builder George Weekes' men off the sea defence work at Totland, with pickaxe handles. A young lad had been watching and suddenly made a dive and went through the black plastic. They asked if they should pursue him. I said, "No, you come with me." I knew what had happened; he went straight through the plastic fence and into *the trench which was about two feet deep and mostly full of piss. It was the gents loo, and the poor sod was soaked, so we decided to leave him be.'*

Refused funding by the Isle of Wight County Council for a public swimming pool on the Island, the people decided to follow the latest trend – even Joe Grundy in *The Archers* tried it – and hold an open air pop concert to raise money. The echo of this decision, magnified beyond belief, was to come back to hit Freshwater, with a vengeance, two years later.

Events at Godshill are less clear: this was the most private of the three festivals, and both press reports and eye-witness accounts are hazy; in brief it seems to have been an Alice-in-Wonderland mixture of the mundane and the bizarre. Certainly a good time was had by all... An audience of 10,000 congregated on forty acres of barley stubble known as Hayles Field – translated by the press into 'Hell Field' – on Ford Farm, near Godshill but nearer Niton, just off the main road from Newport to Ventnor. The event began at 8 pm on Saturday, 31 August and ended at 8.30 the following morning – it was supposed to run from 6 pm to 10 am, so it started late and finished early! Tickets were the grand sum of 25 shillings each, £1.25 in post-decimal (and inflationary) times.

The few tickets that have survived are worth considerably more than their face value! Printed in typically garish psychedelic colours and designed – as was the strange Festival poster – by Dave Roe, who was artist-in-residence for all three festivals, it lists the bands playing on one side, and a bizarre children's story for adults – another sign of the times – on the other.

Dave Roe's poster design is just as baffling, dominated by a German World War I flying ace who has become the head (literally) of his own psychedelic airplane. Headed by the words 'Zooming about with gembral gording', this is slightly more comprehensible than the press advert, which shows three aircraft in motion, one mounted by a bird-headed man who might just be Jefferson. Both posters are topped by an American eagle with the scrolled words, 'To the polls, ye sons of freedom'. All becomes more confusing in that both artworks bill the Crazy World Of Arthur Brown over Jefferson Airplane.

Geoff Wall recalls the sheer excitement of the times.

'We embarked from Southsea on the Ryde-bound ferry – there were so many people about that it resembled something used during the Dunkirk evacuation! To have such a musical feast so close to home was unbelievable, and to see the Airplane live – well it was a dream come true. We caught a tatty bus from Ryde to the Festival site, and what a site!

'The boundary fence consisted of black plastic sheeting – a far cry from the high wooden fences and security guards that accompanied future IOW events. The loos were a simple trench, again surrounded by some plastic bags. The stage itself was just two flatbed trailers placed together, with plastic sheeting covering a makeshift scaffolding structure. To the right of the stage was a huge screen.

'Many people had come just in shirt-sleeves. Unfortunately the temperature dropped late at night, which caused the unprepared crowd to collect what stubble they could, and light fires. Black plastic sheeting was re-used for protective insulation, and high winds blew the smoke straight through the stage and light show. This upset the bands and obscured the vision. But I remember the Airplane were magnificent.'

Publicised as one of the biggest pop festivals ever staged in this country, events got under way early on Saturday evening. After weeks of planning the supposedly highly organised, precision-planned gig turned out to be 'sixteen hours of make-do, make-shift and hasty improvisation'.

Earlier, the 114 musicians arrived in three specially chartered hovercraft; lesser mortals arrived by ferry. A fleet of special buses carried fans to the site, though many walked. The specially erected signposts had been switched round or removed altogether; it is not insignificant in this context to note that the local branch of the National Farmers' Union had earlier expressed worries about livestock on surrounding land! It is also worth remembering that during the previous attempted invasion of the Island's south coast, in 1940, signposts had also been removed, somewhat more officially. Another saboteur cut off the field's telephone by removing fifty feet of cable.

Technical difficulties meant often as much as a half-hour break between each group. Indeed, the Festival seemed dogged by trouble even before it started. Organisers and sponsors associated with it had already disclaimed responsibility for anything that happened 'on the night', and the Island's magistrates hit out at them for advertising bar facilities before they had applied for a licence. Pre-publicity promised 'licensed bars, marquee, refreshments and snack bar'.

The whole arena was illuminated by floodlights – bright enough to show fans where they were going without being too brilliant to spoil the atmosphere. Long refreshment tents at either side of the field were also well illuminated and patronised. The concessionaire, a local Island ice-cream manufacturer, was charging 2/6d for an egg sandwich or a can of coke. He soon lost his monopoly to a freelance fish and chip van and a number of pirate hot dog stalls, who gatecrashed the field.

Power for the lighting and the amplification – which at times proved faulty, causing long gaps between acts – was supplied by a noisy generator. Groups occupied large tents behind the stage when not appearing. At the opposite end of the field, marquees were supplied for the police, security guards, the medical unit and fans requiring shelter. The whole affair was a miniature precursor of Afton, beauty and danger coalescing in a rural setting, with the pop fans like the 'poor bloody infantry' of the Great War, setting out for the trenches. As the *Islander* reported:

> *'Hell's Field was a beautiful setting for the Festival, surrounded by rolling green hills and bright, bright sunshine. There was, however, something ominous about the enclosure: it looked very much like a prison camp, a detention compound. An area all round the billowing black PVC walls was marked off with wire, and patrolled by a Security man holding an alsation on a tight lead. The queue at the entrance was very orderly and seemed unnaturally quiet, almost apprehensive.'*

And so the scene was set; it was obvious that though almost everyone had come to see Jefferson Airplane, no pop festival would be worth the name unless the Beatles were going to put in an appearance. They too were coming to see the Airplane, claimed the organisers... but of course they never did.

Quite who did appear, and in exactly in what order, is still a subject of lounge-bar argument, but the following is the nearest one can surmise about an event now wreathed in mystery. As someone once said, if you can remember the sixties, you weren't really there!

The poster promised Jimmy Saville – who no one can remember being there – and a 'lite-show' by a student of the RCA. Musical director, as at the subsequent festivals, was Rikki Farr, a Portsmouth night club impresario. Local band Halcyon Order – the misspelling was deliberate, not a result of them being thick – opened the proceedings with the drum marathon 'Toad', in the excitement of which Island legend Paul Athey broke his bass drum. They played nine other songs by Cream, and 'My White Bicycle' by Tomorrow for variety.

'Thank you very much, that was definitely Halcyon Order...' said compere and Radio 1 DJ 'Laughing' John Peel, who made a brief appearance to start proceedings. The only thing he could remember, twenty-six years on, was...

> '...one fragile hobitette who was crying because her bare feet were so cold and, overcome with lust, I gave her my socks. She skippety skipped away and that was that. I want my socks back. And I want them washed first, too.'

She probably still treasures them! Next, Peel – a generous man despite his curmudgeonly self-image – introduced his current faves, Tyrannosaurus Rex.

TYRANNOSAURUS REX

'Two little men, squatting amongst a warehouse of amplifiers and mikes', one eye witness declared. They were still in their acoustic heyday, with Steve Peregrine Took on bongos, hand drums and tinker bells and Marc Bolan warbling sagas of elves, magicians and Romany soup – light years away from his pop stardom in the early seventies. As their first LP, curtly titled *My People Were Fair And Had Sky In Their Hair, But Now They're Content To Wear Stars On Their Brow*, had just been released, they demanded the huge fee of £60 for their efforts, and started off proceedings with their typical wayward magic.

Before his early death in a car crash, Bolan sacked the increasingly wayward Took and became a glitter superstar, and an early godfather of punk. Steve Took also died young, choking to death on a cocktail cherry. And yet in 1968 they had the charm, and mystery, of two young gods, harbingers of another world...

JOHN PEEL

John Peel's presence at these events was itself a sort of alternative Good Housekeeping seal of approval; in the hippie hierarchy, he too had god-like status. His pirate radio show *The Perfumed Garden* and subsequently *Top Gear* and *Nightride* on Radio 1, provided the first airing in England of the new West Coast music, and its homegrown imitators, sounds which dominated the 1968 Festival.

There was a time when he was so fashionable that I recall meeting Peel look-alikes! Nevertheless, to the fury of each new wave of rock audiences, Peel has continued to seek out the new and interesting (if sometimes unlistenable) and to abandon the old. Certainly his calming, ironic presence – as compared to the jargon toting, emotional Rikki Farr – was sadly lacking at the two subsequent festivals.

AYNSLEY DUNBAR RETALIATION

A hard driving blues band, they climaxed with 'Rubber Duck', which brought the crowd to its feet. Drummer Aynsley later moved to California, where he played with such luminaries as Frank Zappa, after the 'blues boom' of the time had turned sour.

PLASTIC PENNY

The Plastic Penny were originally an Irish showband called Chris Lamb And The Universals, but when stardom beckoned they recruited two younger musicians, drummer Nigel Olsson – later to play with Elton John – and lead guitarist Mick Grabham who subsequently joined Cochise, then Procol Harum. They came over on the hovercraft with T. Rex, and played a particularly ambitious version of 'Strawberry Fields Forever'. Their next gig was a week's cabaret in Derby.

Things become a little hazy hereabouts. Next up were the Mirage, and folk-rock act Hunter Muskett. The softer end of English psychedelia was well represented by the Orange Bicycle, whose only LP was produced by John Peel and featured songs by the then unknown Elton John.

SMILE

Newly signed to the Apple label, and thus provoking rumours that the Beatles were set for a surprise appearance, it was Smile's first live date, and they played their forthcoming single, a cover of Dylan's 'Please Mrs Henry' – 'if the Manfreds don't step in first'. This was not the only hint of things to come. Named after a double album by next year's headliner, Blonde On Blonde displayed 'exceptional interplay' between their twin lead guitarists.

THE MOVE

Birmingham's finest, the Move, drew much of their live material from West Coast luminaries like Moby Grape (also an early influence on Robert Plant). They played at deafening volume, and blew nine speakers.

Shortly after this performance, they splintered in all kinds of musical directions, like an exploding star. Singer Carl Wayne disappeared into cabaret, while bassist Ace Kefford – the 'singing skull' – disappeared into drug abuse, from which he has only recently re-emerged. Roy Wood and drummer Bev Bevan founded the Electric Light Orchestra, before Wood became a semi-permanent fixture on *Top Of The Pops* with Wizzard, and with an increasingly bizarre hairdo. Trevor Burton – the most menacing figure I have ever seen on a public stage – later joined the Steve Gibbons Band.

The consensus among Islanders later was that the Move stole the show.

THE PRETTY THINGS

Lead guitarist Dick Taylor still remembers the 1968 event warmly.

> *'There was a very friendly atmosphere, almost romantic. I thought it was more special in many respects than the other festivals.'*

The Pretty Things got an enthusiastic welcome, which increased when Twink began climbing all over the scaffolding on stage. They came fresh from the studio, having just recorded *SF Sorrow*, a rock opera which influenced *Tommy*, but remains a sadder, more bitter work. Songs from this project featured in their act, as did their truly demented drummer,

'Twink' and his mime act. They also played 'Alexander' and 'My White Bicycle' (again) from Twink's previous band.

Taylor recalls the truly magical lighting effects that night. 'And that was when we all had our own light show.' Happy days!

The Pretty Things' personnel from this era have recently reformed. Their first public appearance was at the Twenty-fifth Anniversary IOW Music Festival at Smallbrook Stadium, Ryde. This line-up also appeared in the quite bizarre 'psychedelic dungeon' scenes in a Norman Wisdom film, *What's Good For The Goose*. Like all the best British psychedelic bands – the Floyd, Soft Machine, Traffic, Procol Harum, Mighty Baby – their roots were in dirty, sweaty R&B.

JEFFERSON AIRPLANE

Despite all of this homegrown talent, it was the Jefferson Airplane who provided the real highlight of the festivities. They ambled on stage and immediately started to rock.

Lead singers Grace Slick and Marty Balin prowled the stage, their searing harmonies like twin headlights. With additional vocals from guitarist Paul Kantner, their vocal attack remains unparalleled in rock music to this day. Meanwhile, lead guitarist Jorma Kaukonen and bassist Jack Casady – later to form the independent band Hot Tuna – wove instrumental lines of angular virtuosity. The sheer ferocity of the Airplane at this time was almost a physical threat.

It was quite different from anything even hardcore fans had expected. The folky love ballads of *Jefferson Airplane Takes Off* and *Surrealistic Pillow* had been replaced by harder hitting material from the then unreleased *Crown Of Creation* LP. Geoff Wall distinctly remembers being shocked by the vastly revamped version of 'Somebody To Love'.

'Gone was the fast, frantic, driving pace (that I loved on Surrealistic Pillow*) and in its place we were presented with a slower version that I later came to love on* Bless Its Pointed Little Head. *Songs such as 'Watch Her Ride' demonstrated the just what a brilliant rhythm guitarist Paul Kantner was. As for Grace Slick, she was beautiful! I felt she was probably the most splendid creature in the world – and she could sing too!'*

On the huge screen next to the stage, the Airplane's 'lite-show', which they had brought over from San Francisco, displayed ever-changing liquid slides that matched both the mood and moment. They had brought an entourage of thirty lighting technicians and sound experts and five tons of electrical equipment, a revelation for English audiences. As Dick Taylor remembers, 'They used lots of slides. The set looked like a Viking ship.'

Nevertheless, the Airplane's drummer Spencer Dryden – wearing a cowboy hat to combat the cold – was none too happy with the Festival. During their ninety-minute set, none of the group could hear each other, and they were constantly forced to stop and re-tune in an attempt to get a uniform sound. Coupled with this, the group's psychedelic screen show had to be cut right down in case the field's thick covering of dust damaged valuable lens. Despite this, they continued with a static light show – which the *Record Mirror* described as 'their reversed optical illusion projections' – and got easily the best reception of any of the fourteen groups to appear.

The Airplane had already played Brussels and Stockholm on their short European tour, and were to play a few days later at Parliament Hill Fields, another concert to enter the realms of legend. This line-up reformed in 1989, and made a comeback LP, but to paraphrase B.B. King, the thrill was definitely gone.

Ron Smith remembers paying them £1,000 for their performance, which seems the bargain of the century until he mentions that Fairport cost only £80.

ARTHUR BROWN

If the fans had come to see the Airplane, they came to gape at headlining act The Crazy World Of Arthur Brown. With gold mikes and gold masks, and his beanpole height and operatic voice, Arthur was a stalwart of the Middle Earth club, and a pioneer of psychedelia. He had decided to arrive at the Festival by balloon from Portsmouth, but things went amiss and it was cancelled at the last moment. The God of Hell Fire could not summon up the necessary north-westerly wind!

Arthur declared to the crowd 'It's a great atmosphere here!', an atmosphere he rapidly polluted with the smoke bombs at the conclusion of his greatest hit, 'Fire'. Unfortunately, in the cold and damp, Brown's famous flaming headgear failed to ignite, despite his best attempts with a cigarette lighter backstage. One reporter described him as 'ghostlike' – certainly after Brown had finished the fans drifted away in their thousands. Brown remembers his own return, '...flying back on a ratty old cargo plane. Marshall stacks were piled in. Entering an air pocket, they were thrown across on the band.'

Interviewed by the compilers of *Isle Of Wight Rock*, Brown dragged up further memories:

'I could hardly see the audience, and didn't feel terribly connected with them. I was clad in gold. Sometimes it was gold, sometimes red velvet, sometimes black velvet with robes and capes. We did some songs from our album – 'Spontaneous Apple Creation', 'Nightmare'. We also played R&B fare like James Brown's 'I Got Money' and 'I Put A Spell On You'.'

The bad luck that dogged this performance was to continue. The Crazy World Of Arthur Brown – basically Pete Solley on organ and Carl Palmer on drums – soon split up, having failed to secure another hit single. Arthur subsequently formed Kingdom Come – the first rock band to feature a drum machine – and shaved off one side of this hair and beard. He now lives in Texas, though he did recently return for some British gigs, into which he processed like a deranged monk, then began a gradual striptease of endless layers of clothes. His voice can still chill the soul, though.

Carl Palmer played at the 1970 Festival with his new band Emerson, Lake And Palmer, a 'supergroup' whom the original Crazy World – with Vincent Crane on organ and Drachen Theaker on drums – could have blown into the Solent. And so it goes...

FAIRPORT CONVENTION

It was left to Fairport Convention to take on the hardest job of the night. They followed Arthur Brown, to a greatly diminished crowd. Those who stayed slept. So the Convention found themselves playing to a huddled audience of sleeping bags, resembling – according to *New Musical Express* – 'a musical refugee camp'.

This was somewhat of a pity, as this was the classic line-up of the band, with Sandy Denny and Ian Matthews on lead vocals – a gentler counterpart to the Airplane, with whom early Fairport were often compared. Their set included covers of Joni Mitchell's 'Chelsea Morning', Richard Farina's 'Reno Nevada', a Thompson guitar extravaganza, and Leonard Cohen's 'Suzanne', with a 'Bo Diddley Backbeat'.

The group which played in 1968 was an exploding supernova of talent, sparks from which continue to light the horizon. Sandy Denny and drummer Martin Lamble are both – sadly – no more, but Sandy lived long enough to leave a recorded legacy which continues to haunt all those who ever saw her live, and a new generation of folk romantics. There was always something oddly vulnerable about her: Adrian Henri remembers meeting her coming out of the press enclosure in tears the following year because she couldn't get a seat to see Dylan.

Ian Matthews subsequently had a No. 1 hit about another large outdoor festival, 'Woodstock', and moved to America where musically he felt most at home. He met three members of his next band, Matthews' Southern Comfort, at Godshill. Bass player Ashley Hutchings, the Sherpa Tenzing of English folk-rock, founded Steeleye Span and the Albion Band, and continues to reinvent the folk tradition. Richard Thompson went on to a hugely successful solo career. Simon Nicol – the rock, in both senses, on which Fairport was built – continues to lead the current Fairport, and their annual music weekend at Cropredy has much the same friendly atmosphere as the Godshill event.

Fairport's set was reportedly 'majestic'. They were then closer to American folk–rock than to the English folk music they – in more than one sense – electrified, with Thompson's long, curling guitar lines the equal of anything from the West Coast. Out of nervousness, Ian Matthews always sang with his eyes closed.

'I started Leonard Cohen's 'Suzanne' in darkness; when I opened my eyes at the end of the song it was dawn.'

THE CHEROKEES ·

The *New Musical Express* considered their performance was 'well worth a listen' which is particularly remarkable, as although billed and on site they did not actually play. When Fairport finished it was 5.30 am, and everyone had just about had enough. The *Islander* magazine reported that morning light...

'...brought a scene reminiscent of the aftermath of Culloden: survivors standing, bleary and unshaven, wrapped in cloak-like blankets and remnants of PVC.'

Grizzled veterans of all three Island festivals still maintain that this one had the best atmosphere. It was like the secret gathering of a new found religion, the beginning of a quiet revolution...

O pleasant exercise of hope and joy!
For mighty were the auxiliars which then stood
Upon our side, we who were strong in love!
Bliss was it in that dawn to be alive,
But to be young was very Heaven!
Wordsworth: The Prelude, Book XI

Such times will not easily be recaptured.

And so events concluded. Rest days and leave for Island police had been cancelled during the weekend, but the absence of trouble meant that the police, together with the Festival stewards and security men along with their five guard dogs had comparatively little to occupy them. Police were on hand, however, when those present started using chairs to keep the many small fires from going out after orthodox fuel had been expended. In addition, three cars and a motor scooter disappeared during the night, but were all afterwards recovered. Ron Smith recalls:

'After it was all over, my mother had come down on holiday, and with my wife and two daughters we spent more or less the whole of the following week clearing up the site.'

The only damage of note was caused by fans who wandered through a neighbouring field of barley. Mr Corbin, of Holden Farm, told the *Isle Of Wight County Press* that fencing, hedges and the barley itself had suffered, representing between £30 and £40 worth of damage. However, he added that the majority of the damage was accidental and the fans he had met had apologised and were most courteous. Fences broken by spectators created a further problem for Mr Corbin, who spent anxious moments preventing his herd of cattle from wandering through the gaps.

For the thirty St John's Ambulance Brigade members on duty it was one of the busiest nights on record; the complement on duty was the largest number ever used on the Island. Sixty-eight cases – seventy per cent from the mainland – were treated in a tent well-equipped as a medical aid centre with stretcher beds, but only three people needed to be taken to hospital in Ryde – a severe asthma case, a girl whose foot had been run over by a bus and a case of epilepsy.

The main complaints were burns, collapses and cuts – many caused by flying missiles, including beer cans. One girl received five stitches in a head wound. As the night wore on, the biting wind forced several spectators to tear plastic sheeting from the arena's perimeter to wrap themselves in, and one youngster was treated for hypothermia.

Nevertheless, throughout the cold night and early morning rain – prefiguring the end of the 1970 event on 'Sunshine Island' – the fans remained faithful, sitting quietly in the stubble, and patiently awaiting a visitation from the Beatles who never arrived. Indeed, John Lennon and George Harrison would both attend the next year's festival, but in the excitement of the person headlining, an ex folk singer from Minnesota, their presence was to be almost incidental!

2

Dylan: a quest fulfilled

The Godshill event might have remained an interesting footnote to the history of rock in the sixties. It became instead the seed from which two far stranger and more exotic blooms took root, for two reasons. One was the Island itself, long the haunt of poets and mystics – Tennyson's garden isle – which became the natural setting for the 'back to nature' ideology of open air festivals. (It is no coincidence that the Green movement has found a natural home here recently.) The second was the three Foulk brothers – Ray, Ron and Bill. Along with rock promoter Rikki Farr – all four were still only in their early twenties – they had been heavily involved in organising the Godshill event, and under the name Fiery Creations set about putting on a second festival. It was their energy and determination which now went boldly where no one else had dared go before. And the dream came true!

Local rumour has the idea for inviting Bob Dylan emerging from a drinking session in a local Totland hostelry. 'Turner' Smith again:

The next winter, the Foulks said, "We're thinking of having another one, Ron; we're thinking of having Dylan." Ray, who had studied graphic design at Southampton University, put together a beautiful brochure, and said he was going off to the States. We looked at what money we had, and we had enough for Ray's return air ticket, but nothing for him to live on in the States. He went off, with enough cash to get a taxi to Dylan's place, and spoke at the intercom at the gate to Dylan, and Dylan let him in. He stayed there three or four days, and came back with Dylan's agreement to appear at the pop festival, and from then onwards, it was fairly easy.'

Ray Foulk told Chris Hockenhull of the Dylan fanzine *Fourth Time Around* exactly how they went about attaining the impossible.

'In about January 1969, we put an advert in the Isle Of Wight County Press *with a small form to reply on, asking who would people like to see at the next festival. I had not personally thought of Dylan at that time. I don't think anybody had. The response from the newspaper advert was very small. Surprisingly, it didn't produce many big names. We had thought about Elvis, the Beatles, Rolling Stones etc. We put this down, at the time, to the fact that it was beyond people's expectations as to just who would appear at a concert on the Isle of Wight.'*

The search went on to find someone who would headline. Various names continued to be tossed about. Ray Foulk:

'Both Ronnie and I were not terribly well up on the music scene to be honest and I used to take the advice of my younger brother Bill who had come up with a lot of the acts for the '68 Festival. It was Ronnie's department booking acts and he kept throwing names about and kept saying, "What about Bob Dylan... he's a big name, he'll pack them in."'

The immediate response was a straight refusal. Following a mysterious motorcycle accident in July 1966 – in the middle of his cataclysmic world tour with the Hawks – Dylan had gone to ground in Woodstock, and was pursuing a Garbo-like seclusion. He was recording home demos with the same musicians – now renamed the Band – the strange, surrealistic parables which later became known as the *Basement Tapes*: healing music, in which Dylan immersed himself while recovering from white-line fever (of whatever kind). Nevertheless, Ray Foulk had by now warmed to the idea of getting Dylan to headline the Festival, and he was not easily dissuaded.

> '*We hired a camera and one afternoon went around the island shooting various sites. We also produced a booklet virtually overnight titled* For The Attention Of Bob Dylan *listing various details of who was on the bill, lighting and sound details and other information about the Festival. So we came up with the idea of making it a holiday for him and his family, in a farmhouse in Bembridge with a swimming pool and a recently converted barn suitable for rehearsing in. We were offering Dylan a fortnight stay there, no expense spared, car with driver. Also we would have him come over on the* QEII. *The fee offered was $50,000.*'

Meanwhile Fiery Creations were going through the usual problems of contending with protests from islanders who wanted the proposed festival cancelled. Not surprising really, for at the time the Isle of Wight was inhabited by just over 100,000 people, with more than a third over sixty years of age, retired in relative peace and quiet.

The site chosen was Woodside Bay, on the north east facet of the Island's diamond. Access was by a private road, skirting the treelined shoreline which edges Wootton Creek and then winds past mansions and holiday camps to farmland and the Solent. Built on high ground, the arena would command spectacular views over to the mainland. None the less, the event was given the official go ahead.

In June, Dylan was interviewed by Jann Wenner for *Rolling Stone* and the opening question was...

Wenner: When do you think you're gonna go on the road?
Dylan: November... possibly December.

However, on 14 July, Dylan joined the Band on stage at the Mississippi River Festival in Illinois, introduced as Elmer Johnson, and played four songs with them. He then requested a tape of the show to listen to. Dylan must have decided shortly after – if he hadn't already – that he'd do the Isle of Wight, as the *Melody Maker* for 26 July ran the news on its front page 'Dylan here in August', and carried a copy of the telegram from Bert Block confirming Dylan's agreement dated 'Freshwater, IOW 17 July, '69'.

The Foulk brothers contacted Block and found he agreed to the fee offered, on condition that the Band would also perform – their fee being $8,000 – and that another of Block's acts, Richie Havens, would also be added to the bill. Ray Foulk:

'We thought $50,000 (£20,000) for Dylan quite cheap. Block asked me to come over to New York to sort out the contracts. I remember having to sit down, as we then realised we had Dylan. I quickly arranged to go to New York with Rikki Farr.'

The day after the contracts were signed, Foulk and Farr were to meet Dylan at their room at the Drake Hotel. Ray Foulk:

'It was a very brief meeting, only a couple of minutes. He struck me as being a very ordinary person, not what you would imagine such a big star to be like. I think Dylan wanted to see who he was dealing with. I didn't regard it as being any sort of test or interview. Dylan didn't ask us anything really. I regarded the meeting as a real treat.'

Foulk and Farr returned to England to continue to book acts for a three day event to be held at Woodside Bay, Wootton, near Ryde, IOW from 29 to 31 August. It was heralded as Dylan's 'only appearance in the world' with a ticket price of £2.10.0 for the weekend.

It was in the early press announcements of Dylan's appearance that the rumours of a four-hour Dylan set were founded, despite the insistence from Block that it would only be a one-hour performance that would close the Festival on Sunday evening.

Dylan was set to arrive in England two weeks before the concert; he was expected to stay on at Forelands for a few days afterwards. The whole adventure was being presented as a holiday, interrupted by a few hours work. The singer certainly needed to get away; the whole of hippie America seemed to be making for his own back door to attend the upcoming Music And Arts Fair at Woodstock.

Bob Dylan broke his silence – the Isle of Wight appearance was now being labelled as 'The Comeback' in the press – to Don Short of the *Daily Mirror* on 9 August. He admitted that 'It's nice to be back', and added,

'Gee, I'm nervous. I've been so long out of it. But we're gradually getting the show together.'

He revealed that George Harrison had offered him and the Band the use of the Apple studios in London. Dylan stated,

'I'm very happy with the way I've progressed. I think my voice is better now than ever before. I like my new songs too.'

Dylan and Sara with two of their children, Maria and Jesse, boarded the *QEII* in New York for the journey to England. Disaster struck shortly afterwards. Jesse lost consciousness after hitting his head against a cabin door, during a pre-sail party in Dylan's stateroom, and the ship's doctor refused to accept responsibility for the boy's ability to make the voyage. Dylan had little alternative but not to sail. He disembarked, carrying Jesse, only thirty minutes before the ship left dock, and took his son straight to hospital.

Ray Foulk:

'It was dreadful news. I was at this stage in daily contact with Block. He telephoned me with the news that Dylan had left the ship to go to the hospital and was still in New York. Block said that Dylan would obviously have to fly over at a later date. The accident brought home to us the vulnerability of our position. What if the boy had been killed? Dylan would obviously have cancelled. The event all hinged upon this one human being. It shook us up a bit.'

33

Jesse recovered enough for Dylan to feel happy to come to England. The two children would not now accompany him. He arrived at Heathrow Airport late on the evening of Monday 25 August. Bert Block had already visited the Festival site and seemed quite happy with the arrangements. Foulk recalls Dylan's arrival at the airport:

'It was very low key. He arrived on a regular flight at about 10 pm. Sara was with him as well as Al Aronowitz. Block and myself were there to meet them. We drove down to Portsmouth in two cars which took us about two hours. It was nearly 1 am when we arrived at Portsmouth seafront and very cold. There was hardly anybody around and those who were passed Dylan by without a glance. Because of the cold, we were all drinking tea waiting for our hired hovercraft to arrive. I still have this image of Dylan wandering around with his plastic cup of tea from the vending machine in the dark.

'I was in the firing line dealing with Dylan and Block. I wanted to keep Dylan happy... who knows I may get him to work for us again. On the other hand, I was getting word back from our office that ticket sales were slow and we had to get more publicity out of Dylan. I thought that if we could arrange one main press conference rather than set up individual interviews, Dylan may well agree to do it.'

Dylan settled into Forelands. On the Tuesday, George Harrison and friend Mal Evans, an ex Cavern Club 'bouncer', drove to the Isle of Wight. Harrison and wife Patti returned on the Thursday and stayed with the Dylans at Forelands for the rest of Dylan's stay.

Security, while tight was very low key at Forelands Farm. The atmosphere was relaxed. Judy Lewis, drafted in as housekeeper and now married to the English surrealist poet David Gascoyne, recalls the minutiae of those dream days:

'One of the first things Bob asked me to get him was some honey. He was quiet and came over as a very well mannered

person. Most of his time he spent playing guitar with George Harrison. He took a liking for blackberry and apple pies and fruit cakes! Sara was constantly going on at him about his diet. I was forever supplying endless cups of tea to him and Harrison. After supper some evenings he would ask if I would like him to sing something. I would demote George Harrison to go fetch things from the kitchen and help me do the washing up so I would not miss anything.'

Among the songs Judy recalls Dylan performing in the unlikely setting of the dining room were 'Mr Tambourine Man', 'Lay Lady Lay' and 'Blowing In The Wind'. The music Dylan played with Harrison seemed to Judy Lewis to be incomplete songs and instrumentals, which often ended before they got going. She recalls Harrison often saying, 'Play that bit again Bob... What do you think of that bit?'

Ray Foulk:

'I was going over to Bembridge at least once a day. I remember walking through the living room one day and Dylan and Harrison were sitting on a sofa singing the Everly Brothers 'All I Have To Do Is Dream' together. It sounded incredible... just like the Everly Brothers. There was a lot less rehearsal going on there than one may have imagined. He spent much of the time with Harrison sitting on the lawn talking.'

Judy Lewis recalls that Dylan and Harrison spent some time playing tennis: 'I must admit that Dylan wasn't very good at all.' Ringo Starr with his wife Maureen spent a day with the Dylans at the farmhouse. Another guest was John Lennon with Yoko as ever in attendance. Ray Foulk, again:

'Lots of helicopters were landing by and using a field next to the farmhouse and then the visitors would make their way across the field into the grounds of Forelands. The grounds were well kept by a gardener and were immaculate. Then this helicopter appeared and flew over. However, it didn't put down in the

field like the rest but landed right down on the lawn blowing all the flowers away much to the rage of the gardener. Out of the helicopter strolled John Lennon.'

By the middle of the week the press had arrived in large numbers on the Island, concentrating their reporting on the invading horde of hippies, and on the reported fee which Dylan was to receive. Ray Foulk's idea of holding a one-off press conference at last bore fruit. It took place at the Halland Hotel, Seaview, on Wednesday afternoon, 27 August. Dylan arrived with Ray Foulk, Al Aronowitz, Bert Block, Mal Evans and Rikki Farr.

Two members of the Band, Robbie Robertson and Rick Danko, were already present, as were publicist Les Perrin – famous for his 'two telephone' technique as immortalised in the film of Dylan's 1965 concert tour, Don't Look Back – and Fiery Creations publicity supremo Peter Harrigan. Dylan has always reserved some of his finest performances for the press, misinformation raised to high art. This example proved, in some ways, more entertaining than Dylan's somewhat low energy performance at the Festival itself, which could have been prefigured in a couplet from 'Blonde On Blonde': *The country music station plays soft/but there's nothing, really nothing to turn off'*.

The 'voice of his generation' proved equally difficult to draw out of his shell, the greatest living poet acting tongue-tied!

Press: Why did you come to the Isle of Wight?
Dylan: I wanted to see the home of Alfred, Lord Tennyson.
Press: Why?
Dylan: Just curious.
Press: Can I have your general views on the situation of drug taking among teenagers and young people these days?
Dylan: I don't have any of those views... I wish I did, I'd be glad to share them with you, but I... I think everyone should lead their own lives you know.
Press: You used to, I believe, make public pronouncements on your views on things like Vietnam, and it has been noticed in certain quarters you haven't been doing this recently, making your views

known on big political and international issues. Is this deliberate policy on your part?

Dylan: No... I think that's more a rumour than a fact. You check your old newspapers, you won't be able to find too many statements I've made on these issues.

Press: I've heard it said here today by some of your fans that the new Bob Dylan is a bit of a square... is that true?

Dylan: You'll have to ask the fans. [Amidst general laughter.]

Press: Do you feel that your days of protesting are over?

Dylan: I don't want to protest anymore... I never said I am an angry young man.

Press: Can you tell us exactly what happened when you suffered an accident a while ago?

Dylan: Rikki... where are you...? [Silence from Dylan for a moment.] It's true I suffered a broken neck. It's awful hard to explain. I have to take it easy sometimes.

Press: Bob?

Dylan: Yes, Ken. [General laughter from press.]

Press: Do you think you have changed very much since we last saw you in London? Your clothes and hair have changed.

Dylan: I believe there's a conscious thing since the accident. I haven't really changed... it had more to do with the show I was doing than anything else. It really had nothing to do with me personally... that stuff was for publicity. I don't do that kind of thing anymore.

Press: Can you tell us what songs you will be performing?

Dylan: Everything we will do is on record. I'm not going to do anything new... things you will have heard before but with new arrangements.

Press: Because of your lack of public appearances, do you still like doing shows?

Dylan: We appeared a month ago in St Louis... the more shows the better.

Press: Who are you looking forward to meeting while you're around?

Dylan: I'm hoping to meet anyone who's around. I'd like to meet the Who and maybe Georgie Fame...

Press: What about the Beatles?

Dylan: George Harrison has come to visit me. The Beatles have asked me to work with them. I love the Beatles and I think it would be a good idea to do a jam session.

Press: What about reports that various people will perform with you on stage?

Dylan: Great, great.

Press: Do you feel that cameras are like guns?

Dylan: I don't know.

Press: Do you feel this change that has come over you and your music is due to domestic effects? Are you chiefly a family man now?

Dylan: I would think so.

Press: There is a very large crowd expected here for your performance. Any comments on that?

Dylan: I just hope it's a good show.

Press: Do you have a personal message for the kids of today?

Dylan: Take it easy and do your job well.

Press: What exactly then is your position on politics and music?

Dylan: My job is to play music. I think I've answered enough questions.

Dylan watched a clip from this press conference on television that evening. He watched it impassively, then told Judy Lewis that he would far rather see Rowan and Martin's *Laugh In*, his favourite television show. For the rest of the week, Dylan either lazed around the grounds of Forelands or continued rehearsing. One afternoon he went sailing with Sara. Another visit was to Osborne House – Queen Victoria revisited – and on Judy Lewis's recommendation Dylan went to hear the monks chanting at Quarr Abbey.

As was Dylan's way, Mrs Lewis suddenly found herself no longer required. The *Sunday People* later ran an article entitled 'Why Dylan Fired Pillar Of Society', stating the reasons as too much 'good time friendliness' and her habit of putting 'Help Bob Dylan Sink The Isle Of Wight' stickers on Dylan's car and all around the farmhouse!

However, she was soon back in the fold, and recalls that on the Saturday, Dylan and the Band ran through their complete repertoire in the barn at Forelands, playing for over four hours. A legend that Dylan and chums popped into a local hostelry, the Crab And Lobster, and started an impromptu jam session has proved groundless. The 'Red Rocking Chair' tape was in fact a scam invented by Island record dealer and trickster Jeff Lewis in a letter to *Let It Rock*.

Conversely, Richard Manuel, in a 'very juiced' state did turn up at the *Medway Queen*, an old paddlesteamer now beached for good on the Medina river, and jammed with the bar band. Garth Hudson preferred to practice alone in the dark in the barn. As his chauffeur put it, 'He'd rather do that than be out on the piss with the lads.'

Dylan's espousal of Victorian values also tended towards tender domesticity. George Harrison had even initiated the American superstar into that terribly English habit of taking his wife tea in bed. Judy Lewis again:

> *'Bob continually ate my porridge and pies with relish. I think Harrison was in awe of him. They got on very well, but I got the impression that Dylan felt Harrison was a bit pushy... wanting to play all of the time. It was funny, looking back, the way I demoted George to help wash up and fetch and carry things, but I felt it was Bob who should get all the attention.*
>
> *'I remember one day Bob asked to have a bath. I said yes of course he could. He said, "Well there isn't anything there to put as a plug." I then remembered that for some reason there was only one plug between all the bathrooms... I told him Bert Block was having a bath at the time and to wait a minute. I then rushed up and banged on the bathroom door and Block's face appeared. I told him, "Can you give me your plug please." He said, "My what?" I said, "Your bath plug please, you've had it for ages... Bob wants a bath."'*

By mid-afternoon on Sunday, the entourage at Forelands was packing up ready to leave for the Festival site. Dylan, Sara and Ray Foulk set off in a Ford transit van. With no police escort, and with Dylan sitting in the front seat, they drove right in among the crowds, and up to the backstage entrance.

Dylan passed the time chatting to John Lennon and Yoko – as well as other assembled Beatles – relaxing in his caravan and showing no sign of nervousness despite the seemingly endless wait for the Band to start their set. Meanwhile, back in the real world, things were a little different...

3

1969 – Wootton: the return of the pop messiah

Outside the cosy and protected confines of Forelands Farm, the pop world had gone bananas. Its house magazine, the *Melody Maker*, traced every new development with the avidness of holy writ.

On 2 August, Ray Foulk displayed a politician's skill at stirring up publicity, appropriate for a man who was running the IOW branch of CND when still a teenager. The whole of America, he claimed, was 'up in arms' over Bob Dylan's forthcoming Festival appearance. 'We have many applications from Americans for tickets, and some people are chartering planes to fly over specially for the concert.'

Foulk discounted stories – probably planted by Fiery Creations itself – that Dylan might appear elsewhere. 'We hold rights for the exclusive appearance of Dylan. Any rumours that he may appear at Hyde Park are false.' Meanwhile ticket applications were flooding in, with 5,000 requests for tickets in the week after news of Dylan's appearance first broke. An attendance of at least 100,000 people was already projected to 'help Dylan sink the Isle of Wight'.

Plans were still in place for a two-day event. As an indication of Dylan's financial worth, tickets for Sunday afternoon – when he and the Band would top the bill – were £2. Attendance on Saturday would cost a mere 25 shillings for an all-day concert, or only ten bob extra for a weekend ticket to see the Who, Moody Blues, Joe Cocker and nine other top-line acts.

Booking the Beatles to appear was beyond even Fiery Creations' wiles. However, on 9 August, Ray Foulk announced the next best thing, that John Lennon had been invited to attend the Dylan concert. A spokesman for Apple commented that, 'John and Yoko are still recovering from the effects of their recent car crash and are not accepting any engagements. We cannot confirm anything at present.'

There was already talk of holding an extra concert on Friday night. Fiery Creation's offices in Totland were already inundated with ticket applications. 'We've had 2,000 letters this morning alone,' said Ray Foulk. 'To date we have received 10,000 applications. And half of the eighty-one shops around the country who are handling tickets are already sold out.'

A week later, Foulk kept the pot stirred by announcing another exclusive. 'Bob Dylan is writing special material for this historic appearance at the IOW. And it is more than likely that his next LP will feature tracks recorded "live" during the event.' The site at Woodside Bay had been extended to one hundred acres, and 'everyone will be able to get a good view'. Special ticket agencies had now been set up in New York, Melbourne, Sydney, Tokyo and Libya, and it was expected that the total number of people converging on the Isle would be around 200,000 – nearly three times the local population!

By now the Friday evening concert had been confirmed, with local groups and folk artists providing a free show earlier that afternoon. On 23 August, a week nearer D Day – Dylan Day? – Fiery Creations announced a further expansion of the site, so that tickets were still available. To broadcast to the growing multitude, WEMs would be supplying a 2,000 watts PA system which was claimed to be the biggest ever used anywhere in the world.

To extend the World War II metaphor, British Rail was preparing for what a spokesman described as 'a second Dunkirk' and would be sending boats from all over the south coast to ferry up to half a million fans to the Isle.

The Band were now to play for an hour on their own, as well as backing Dylan. Richie Havens would arrive on 30 August and Tom Paxton on the 28th. Nice had postponed their American visit in order to appear, while the Who had promised the organisers some 'nice surprises'. Joe Cocker was to fly in especially from the States. The *Melody Maker* surpassed itself in hype. 'The supergroup to end all supergroups' – George Harrison, the Rolling Stones, Blind Faith and Bob Dylan on stage together – could be the grand finale to this weekend's IOW Festival. An unnamed spokesman for the Festival revealed that...

> *'George Harrison has been in touch with Bert Block, of Dylan's management office, saying he would like to take part in a session with Dylan – with Dylan's approval, of course. Blind Faith are flying in from Honolulu after asking if they could appear too. And Jack Bruce has also said he would be ready and willing to join them all on stage. The Rolling Stones – except for Mick Jagger – are staying on Keith Richard's yacht off the Island, and it is understood that they also have expressed a wish to take the stage with Dylan after his performance.'*

By Monday 25 August, over 500 fans were already camping on the Festival site – including American students who had built a wooden hut and named it 'Desolation Row' after the Dylan song.

Ian Lewis, of the Preston Bob Dylan Society, captured the sense of pilgrimage. One of his friends even left home for good to attend!

> *'I set off on the Monday morning before the Festival. My first lift took me to Manchester, then another to just north of London. From there I started to walk; I spent the night in a park shelter. Next night I landed up in Green Park, near the Palace; the park was full of people sleeping rough.'*

In those days it was by choice! Ian then took the train to Portsmouth.

'There was no Dylan on the juke-box so I put on the Nice playing 'America'. I felt I had walked from America! The ferry was packed, people were sleeping on the floor, everybody had a rucksack and a sleeping bag, smoking Woodbines, talking about what Dylan would play. The feeling was that we were part of something very special.'

The Festival site had now been doubled in size and the organisers announced that tickets would now be on sale at the Festival gate. There was sufficient room to ensure that none wishing to go to the Festival need be disappointed. A local scout group put up tents for the homeless, and people pooled food. Ian Lewis still remembers a large communal pot of baked beans, bubbling on an open fire. 'Everyone was so friendly.'

The media was also on the move. Television and radio crews from all over the Continent were heading for the IOW – and Sweden, France and Germany were among those who would be carrying the music live. More to the point, the stage was now in place. Ron 'Turner' Smith again:

'We had Bill Foulk, who was at the RCA, join us, and he had grandiose ideas about designing a mammoth stage and massive gateways to the arena. I did some figures on the ergonomics, when he had this gateway up, and pointed out that the audience would never get through. It was pretty, but would take about four hours for people to get in and out, so it wasn't on.

'Suddenly the stage started to give at the top; the front beams – constructed out of linked scaffold poles – started to sag. I got a digger across to the site, and he stuck his bucket up and managed to get it underneath, to stop the stage collapsing. We strengthened it, and altered the design somewhat, and Bill was nearly crying, but we managed to save the day. If you look

closely at the photographs, there is a kink in the facia of the stage.

'I remember giving up my seat to a couple of the Beatles, and also seeing Dylan at the back of the stage, in his enclosed area which he wouldn't have anyone else in, with his boozing partner, our security chief. There was a fantastic feeling there.

'We didn't have too many problems; the lanes were really overgrown, we had a couple of tractor-driven hedge trimmers going for a couple of days, and filled in the big pot holes in the road. Ronnie Philips, the farmer, had sold the gravel on his land, so there were big holes everywhere, filled with rubble. Some we had to cover over with topsoil so that people could pitch their tents safely.

'A Frenchman was sleeping on the ground and a car came along and ran over him. He was stuck under the back wheels, so I got my fellows round and we lifted the car up and dragged him out. He just had a few marks on his chest, yet he was screaming he was dying, so we got the St John's ambulance over, and he was perfectly alright. It was miraculous.

'We had a demonstration van which I fetched down from Leicester, which we used as the site office. A local solicitor's daughter had asked me for a job, and worked there as my PA assistant. She had been a very introvert person up 'til then, and she developed immensely; her father always used to comment afterwards what a marvellous change it had brought on her; she became a lively, extrovert person.

'We had a junkie go a bit round the bend, and he threatened to kill her. I went in and calmed him down; he had a knife, but we took that off him, and I got the police, who took him away.'

To cope with over twice the Island's usual population, the Festival organisers had created on site an electric, inflatable city. Its delights were very much of the time, Richard Neville's *Playpower* as interpreted by Marshall McLuhan, with architecture by Buckminster Fuller. If McLuhan's concept of a global village became tinged along the way with the paranoid surrealism of Patrick McGoohan's Village in *The Prisoner* – the guards were real enough – this too was all part of the process.

To keep the inhabitants occupied, there were innumerable fringe activities. John Masara from Mushroom Multimedia, who had just participated in an international pornographic exhibition in Sweden, staged a series of happenings involving 100,000 cubic feet of Krazy Foam, with twenty balloons each twenty feet in diameter and 500 feet of polythene tubings two feet in diameter. These were known as 'pneumatic plastic environments', and a good time was had by all.

In a similar fashion, Anthony Scott's Swizpricks were huge, plastic balloons that slowly inflated over the Festival period until – coinciding with the performance of the Who – they reached their full measure of a hundred feet and ejaculated foam and tinsels into the spotlit night air. The 'climax' was reached when they exploded gently into flame, their low hydrogen content burning in an orgy of self-destruction.

Again, Roger Dixon's Car Jousts involved five old autos decked with neon tubing, polyurethane foam, inflatable tubing, sheet metal, bells and cardboard appendages with the drivers dressed as Roman gladiators. Over the Festival weekend – like a nightmare straight from the pages of J.G. Ballard – the five cars were involved in a slow, ritualistic fight to the death.

One of the most sensuous treats of the Festival was the crazy foam machine. Photos of semi-naked revellers enjoying its delights zapped around the world, an image which captured the sexy innocence of the times. A special device – like an exploding washing machine – blew out gallons of soapsuds, a thick white foam which undulated in the wind, into which people hurled themselves, rolling, kissing, dancing and generally acting like berserk children – or like 'strange snowmen', as the journalist Polly Toynbee described them.

Other delights included the Festival cinema in a large marquee housing up to 400 people, light shows by Black Sun, local folk and blues singers performing in the big top, a non-stop discothèque and poetry readings by, among others, Christopher Logue, Edward Lucie-Smith and Anthony Haden-Guest.

Logue recalls being met by Robert Cotton, 'a young man brimming with good nature', and being introduced to Farr (black sombrero, big shoulders, confident lope) and Ronald Foulk ('The Boss', twenty-two, blond, delicate who as the weekend blossomed retired into a harassed gloom), then led straight on stage.

'I was heard all over the field in silence and with modest applause. If I didn't bring the field down, at least I made the Guinness Book Of Records.'

To serve other appetites, a service area on-site provided food and drink twenty-four hours a day, along with shops stocking everything from fresh fruit to joss-sticks, and groceries to the latest import LPs. Accommodation was provided by two large camp sites and a big-top marquee – ninety feet in diameter – fitted with ground sheets.

Christopher Logue captured the scene with a poet's sharpness of eye.

'Imagine a seventy-acre field bounded on three sides by lanes. Under normal circumstances a dell sheltering a polite holiday camp forms its fourth, eastern side; for the time being this retreat has been separated by a line of pavilions centred on a long, fifteen foot high stage whose wings support triple banks of loudspeakers, topped with cut-out gods nailed to a hardboard pediment.'

The back of the stage was faced with huge plywood sheets, topslung at both ends (like hangar doors) towards whose opening were a pair of ramps broad enough to take a large van. This allowed the Third Ear band, say, to off-load their violins, tambours and lutes on one side, while the Bonzo Dog Doo-Dah Band loaded their cymbals, exploding robots and giant masks on the other.

Logue recalls an enormous man smothered with tattoos escorting an old lady holding a large carrier bags stuffed to the brim with pound notes.

The man: Bloody ridiculous.
Mr Farr: Stuff it in the boot, mother.

Logue also compares the celebrity enclosure, 'choked with free-loaders, sponging aristos and all the velveteen parasites star groups carry in their rucks' with the open field, where 'the thousands were grouped in knots, sharing food, daydreaming, playing chess, patience, knitting and reading'. He provides a wonderful image of the audience, viewed from the stage.

> *'Seventy acres of people is no mean sight, multi-coloured, casually disposed, moving across one another, resettling themselves and emanating a confident hum. Their undulating surface reminded me of floral silk. When a famous group completed a set, the applauding hands gathered light, and reflections as bright as those from Seurat's Honfluer seascapes came up towards the stage.'*

Fans sat on their sleeping bags all day so as not to lose their places. Others slept in the open. Polly Toynbee described how,

> *'...at night the encampment that slopes down from the arena glitters with thousands of fires. People curl up to sleep by them, some playing quietly on guitars and harmonicas.'*

There were two opposing views as to the ambience thus created. For *Rolling Stone* magazine, Michael Gray was jaundiced to the point of prejudice. Even so, elements of his account certainly ring true, and would crack any rose-tinted glasses now trained on these events from a safe distance of twenty years or more.

> *'At Woodside Bay Dylan came, no longer as a contemporary, the wicked messenger, but as Moses come down from the Mount. This was the essential relationship between him and his audience – and there was no hint that this was extravagant. On the contrary, the more inconvenient it was to get there, the*

more essential it was to make the journey. And most people had a hard time concealing the radiant pride they felt in the achievement – the sense of having served the master well.

'*Life in the town of Ryde became almost a rehearsal for peaceful takeover. Everyone watched 200,000 mirror images acting out their chosen roles. The walk down to the site on Friday afternoon, in a rare hour of sunshine, was an eerie recreation of that scene in The Grapes Of Wrath where the Joads approach the work camp, still optimistic, and are puzzled and then apprehensive because of the line of unhappy-looking people coming away in the opposite direction.*

'*The site looked like a sinister internment camp thinly disguised as an underground Butlin's. At the end of the dirt-track approach, the first view of the arena itself was of twin towers, a closed gate, a high fence with wiring carrying 2,600 volts and long lines of submissive, uncomfortable people. There were queues to filthy mobile bogs, even at four o'clock in the morning.*

'*Up on stage Rikki Farr spent three days imposing his sanctimonious assumed personality onto "you people who really count"... "People, with the fibres of your body, welcome onto the stage the incredible, beautiful Moody Blues."*

'*On the other side of the barrier, there was the press and the nasty pop aristocracy. Grossman, the only one with style, was there, detached and powerful, dismissing the rumours of a supergroup jam session after the Dylan performance. "Of course the Beatles would like to play with Dylan," he said. "I would like to go to the moon."*'

The following article, from an unnamed North of England provincial paper, puts the opposite view; indeed so favourable was it that the 1970 Festival programme reprinted it as a kind of statement for that, still greater event. For all its over-exuberance, it sums up the weekend – and the era – far more realistically than Gray's cynicism. Better rose-tinted spectacles than dark shades which blot out the sun altogether!

'*For three days, this beautiful, reserved island in the Solent had throbbed from coast to coast to the sound of blues, folk and pop music. And when it was all over, the invaders left as peacefully as they had arrived. The Islanders were stunned. How could all those thousands of teenagers pack together without riots, without even a trace of trouble? Quite simply, they were there to hear music. In secluded Woodside Bay at Wootton Creek, near Ryde, they settled down to do just that. People had flocked from Australia, New Zealand, America and the Continent. "Hippie" hitch-hikers took the roads to Portsmouth from all parts of England, Wales and Scotland. Their enthusiasm stirred British Rail, which ran a twenty-four hour shuttle service of ferries to the Island. From Ryde, a bus to Wootton, then like pilgrims to the promised land, up the narrow dusty paths to the Festival site.*

'*Hidden in the trees was Festival City – a canvas community of shops, restaurants and snack bars, where you could buy most things from joss-sticks to hot meals. And in the camping area you could take a stroll through Desolation Row, Little Hilton and the Corner Drugstore – all mini shanty towns of tents, corrugated iron or anything that would make a roof. This was home for the hippie population. They were Festival Citizens, dressed in bowler hats, top hats, striped blankets, tattered jeans and headbands.*

'*They showed respect and tolerance. As one hippie said, "I don't know anywhere else where you could put something down in a crowd, come back, and find it still there."'*

This is far truer to the spirit of things than Gray; the tone was set in the Festival programme. Again designed by Dave Roe, its cover – like the extremely rare Festival poster – shows King Kong surmounting an Empire State Building gone psychedelic. Kong is brandishing a red rose, and has sprouted yellow wings, though his expression is hardly 'peace and love', closer to some of the anarcho-hippies in 1970.

On the inside cover, a school photograph has merged into a cross between Sergeant Pepper and Monty Python, at its centre the aviator from the 1968 poster, and a juke-box. Underneath come the dedications, with 'a very special thanks to mother' and to such helpers as 'garibaldi, marshmallow, merlin and atomic cotton and partner', not to mention 'farmer philips', the owner of Wootton Farm and therefore the IOW version of Max Yasgur.

Just as Woodstock was imagined into existence by a tightly bonded group of young New Yorkers, the Isle of Wight festivals arose from a specific community of young people living in and around Totland. Before their mother was widowed, the Foulk brothers had lived in Derbyshire in a manor house with grounds laid out by Capability Brown. Ronald A. Foulk and Raymond I. Foulk are listed as brother directors, with J.P. Foulk responsible for 'festival design', and Jo Foulk 'sales management'. Philip Norman records later the private language the brothers and their helpers spoke, an olde-world north country English full of oratund circumlocutions. Nobody goes anywhere, for example, he 'repairs', while Peter Bull was always referred to by his full name.

The same gang of local – and loyal – retainers masterminded all three festivals. There was the godfather, Brummie Ron 'Turner' Smith, who as a county councillor invented the Countryside Management unit and the Historic Gardens Trust, masterminded a Tennyson Festival and helped preserve two major Victorian buildings – Ryde Pavilion and Dimbola Lodge – from demolition. Peter Bull was also a film maker, and press and public relations supremo Peter Harrigan also taught in Nigeria. His assistant at the time, the very young Bob Cotton is now a pioneer in interactive CD-ROM. Judy Lewis's son Milo, who helped sell tickets, now tours the world with Elvis Costello. Victor Lewis (no relation), the head of security, watched over all three festivals, and still runs Sightguard, the major home security firm on the Island, twenty-seven years on.

However big the festivals got, this 'extended family' serviced and nourished them, and gave them their downhome character. However aggravating he became, even Rikki Farr seemed painfully honest.

As Altamont and – in a different way – Afton were later to show, the back-up security employed by Fiery Creations, though irksome to some hippie values, at least ensured the protection of those wealthy enough to get through the gates. And in those far-off, happy days, when the Welfare State was still in place, that included just about everybody. It would be unfair to say that the whole Festival was simply leading up to Dylan's Sunday night concert, but his approaching appearance hung over the whole weekend.

Festival Log

July to August 1969

5 July, 1969
Hyde Park, London
A free festival to welcome the Rolling Stones' new guitarist, Mick Taylor, and – as events transpire – to mourn his predecessor Brian Jones. The Stones are supported by King Crimson, Family, and the Battered Ornaments. The concert was filmed and released under the name *The Stones In The Park*.

3–6 July, 1969
Newport Jazz Festival
Rhode Island
The first major rock presence at this event, including Led Zeppelin, Ten Years After, Jeff Beck, Jethro Tull and soul legend James Brown.

15–17 August, 1969
Woodstock Music And Arts Fair
New York State
A cast of thousands, including Hendrix, the Who, Crosby, Stills and Nash, Jefferson Airplane, Janis Joplin, Joan Baez, Joe Cocker, Country

Joe, John Sebastian et al, along with 400,000 spectators. Pressure of numbers makes the organisers declare it a free festival half way through. This, and the hugely successful film of the event, will have an enormous effect on next year's Island festival, not least in the booking of many of the same acts.

29–31 August, 1969
Second Isle of Wight Festival
Wootton
The entrance of Mr Bob Dylan and friends.

4

Friday 29 August, 1969

In the words of the *Melody Maker*, 'This was the day of Nice and Bonzos, stalwarts of groupdom, who could be relied on to banish thoughts of creeping rheumatism, aching bladders and claustrophobia, the great plagues of pop festivals.' Fiery Creations now had so much talent at their disposal that they transferred several acts to the Friday night as a free concert.

The Foulks had not been idle since booking Dylan. As a kind of dry run for the Festival, they put on bands at a pub half way between Sandown and Shanklin – the Manor House, Lake – under the name Middle Earth at the Manorhouse. The club only ran from late May to early July, but it remains a legend in Island music circles. Any connection with the original Middle Earth in Covent Garden is, to say the least, obscure.

Ray Foulk used to play Al Bowlly records at half time, and had managed to get his hands on a stroboscope, for psychedelic lighting. Many of the bands he booked subsequently turned up at the Wootton

Festival – the Pretty Things, Free, Marsha Hunt, and Nice. But now it was time for the big league. Marsupilami!

MARSUPILAMI

In the morning and afternoon, there were film shows, 'provincial groups and folk singers from all over Britain', presumably the kind who couldn't even get a paid gig on the *Titanic*. The tough task of opening the Festival on Friday evening fell to Marsupilami, who gave a good account of themselves, and set the Festival off on a solid foundation. Drummer Mike Fourace phoned me years later to give the full story.

They were interlopers! Their manager had reckoned an appearance would boost their image, so they simply turned up in an old transit van, blagged themselves onto the stage, and even ended up being paid. A baffled organiser apologised for having lost the details of their contract. A heavy rock band with keyboards and flute, Marsupilami got lost in the pack, and after releasing two LPs to public indifference, they split up. The Isle of Wight gig was their finest hour.

Rikki Farr now strode on stage for the first of many public announcements:

> *'People if you want to hear more of anyone, you just shout and I'll get them back here for you.'*

ECLECTION

Eclection did indeed earn themselves an encore with their fine mixture of folk, blues and gospel, led by black vocalist Dorris Henderson. Their three-part harmonies soared over the arena like a latter day Mamas And Papas, counterpointed by John 'Poli' Palmer on vibes and drummer Gerry Conway, while Traffic drummer Jim Capaldi joined for part of the set on congas.

The programme explained the group's name was a Joni Mitchell derivation from the adjective eclectic – meaning 'a gathering together'.

*'Between numbers Trevor tells fairy stories in his own
inimitable way and Dorris philosophises and on rare
occasions the road manager gets on stage and sings 'Splish
Splash'.'*

Australian singer Trevor Lucas went on to found Fotheringay with his
wife Sandy Denny, and then they both (re)joined Fairport, or
'Fotheringport Confusion' as Linda Thompson cruelly but accurately
named them. Georg Hultgreen changed his name to George Kajanus,
and formed pop band Sailor. They had one minor hit, then drowned in
a sea of public indifference.

Eclection were something else. Dorris Henderson was already a
legend in the folk clubs of Soho, and their live performances of this
time had a fluidity and strength never captured on record.

BONZO DOG DOO-DAH BAND

From such beauty, the Bonzos provided a rude awakening. Their act
took in spectacular lighting effects, explosions and an odd piece of
hardware which blew hundreds of soap bubbles over the arena. Songs
like 'Monster Mash', 'Canyons Of Your Mind' and 'Urban Spaceman'
had the crowd crying for more. Traffic drummer Jim Capaldi played
drums for part of the set.

The Bonzos were wonderfully funny, while even more chaotic than
usual. Roger Ruskin-Spear's explosives were infuriatingly unreliable
owing to damp fuses and Legs Larry was late owing to a non-starting
taxi driver. Viv Stanshall kept up a running commentary on star arrivals
to the Festival, including the information that Bert Weedon was
tunnelling from Middlesborough and was now believed to be under
the Irish Sea.

A story thing by Vivian Stanshall – souvenir programme

*'The "boys" got together about four years ago at The Royal
College of Art. Fate played the straight man; apart from the*

Curator of Fish who "sat in" now and then. The group was called Bonzo Dog at first, and policy was simply to play as loudly and as badly as possible. It was considered smart to grow a big beard and drink pints of hydrogen peroxide.

'Normally, several of the cranks would set up in a pub and ask for "requests". Nobody could play their instruments, nobody knew the words or the tune (or wanted to) and in any case this wasn't the idea. The "requests" were destroyed. It was great fun. Quite surprisingly, people actually liked it and the audience played to larger and larger boys. Regarded as avant-garde and progressive the band found itself not hated, as hoped for, but something of a legend.

'Soon they had played at nearly every London art school, and their manager, a happy-go-lucky Dick Van Dyke character, started getting work in the provinces. He had a tobacconists... Look, why are you reading this muck? You know it's going to be the same old pretentious drivel... they were working six nights a week (I bet you've got long hair and beads and stuff)... of the original chaos and cacophony... (What's your bag?)... rudeness and riot, some kind of... (Do you play blues harp? I think I dug you down the Earth once)... McCartney a bunch of fives. What a night that... (Can you dig Stevie, Man? Where, Man? Over there, Man. Oh Yeah, Man)... as props, bits of badly designed furniture, vulgar magazines, posters, paintings and sometimes even the smelly contents of... (Spaced out, Man. Done his brain in)... a release from the pressures of study... (out of his box, Man)... theatrical outlet for self-expression... (Can't handle it, Man)... in the nude. Creating noise machines for stage was... (Keep on trucking). The "boys" were also blah, bore, gas etc. (Keep on trucking) Quack, quack.'

This is very close in tone to the paranoia of the Bonzos rock opera *Keynsham*, released the next year. Parts of Stanshall's Festival routine cropped up in the immortal *Radio Flashes*, which he hosted on Radio 1 a few years later.

Viv Stanshall, the greatest radio comic since Hancock, continued to add to the *Rawlinson End* saga until his death in 1995, after a house fire in Crouch End. Neil Innes went on to work with the Monty Python team, as well as making a spoof film on the Beatles, or The Rutles. Meanwhile, Legs Larry tap-danced his way into a million hearts, and Ruskin Spear performed solo – with a team of robots – and released an EP on the theme of wardrobes. Truly, as Chris Welch once wrote, 'they were momentous times, when Bonzos walked the Earth'.

NICE

The performance of the evening. It seemed incredible in those more innocent times that a three-man group could produce such sounds. They concluded with their electric treatment of the Intermezzo from the *Karelia Suite* by Sibelius, booming over the creek in the first hour or Saturday morning. Each instrument, despite the tremendous volume of noise, was clear, and they served up a straight set of hard playing, concluding with Keith Emerson's furniture removing drama for two Hammond organs, to great gusts of applause. A trained classical virtuoso who now dressed in skin tight leather, he would play his organ from the back, or stick knives into it, or straddle it like a bucking bronco. Many performances also ended with the ritual burning of the American flag.

Drummer Brian Davison was compared by many to Ginger Baker, while bassist Lee Jackson added hoarse vocals to the overall mix. Nice had originally been P.P. Arnold's backing group. After they split, Davison founded Every Which Way, and Jackson founded Jackson Heights, both of whom recorded LPs, and both of whom disappeared without trace.

Emerson went on to form one of the first supergroups, Emerson Lake And Palmer, who gave their first major performance at the 1970 Afton event. He never bettered Nice's first LP – with guitarist David

O'List – or their hit single 'America', where the *West Side Story* song became an instrumental attack (literally) on the Vietnam War, or his performance here.

5

Saturday 30 August, 1969

By Saturday afternoon, the mass exodus from the mainland was under way – in ferries, speedboats and even canoes. The Festival site, a short walk from Wootton village – up the west bank of the creek – was already packed. People and tents thronged the approaches; indeed one newly colonised shanty town even named itself 'Desolation Row'. The atmosphere was chaotic, but friendly – even the few uninspired acts drew warm applause.

GYPSY
King Crimson – who had formed across the water in Bournemouth as Giles, Giles And Fripp – were booked to open, and appeared in the official programme, but did not play. It was down to Leicester band Gypsy to open the day's proceedings at 2 pm. *International Times* predicted the following:

> '*When Family were the Roaring Sixties, and played efficient soul music, a group called Le Gay were struggling against overwhelming odds to get into what, I suppose, you call*

progressive music: now they're very much together, have changed their name to Gypsy, and will probably be enormous this summer.'

It was not to be. In the natural selection process of future rock dinosaurs, Gypsy – a perfectly competent but uninspiring country rock band – left few memories. Whereas...

BLODWYN PIG

Blodwyn Pig refuse to die: a modern version still shakes the boards, with Mick Abrahams' trademark guitar extravagance 'Cat's Squirrel' still clocking in at fifteen minutes or so. The original line-up scored a 'signal success', and walked an interesting line between blues and jazz. Abrahams had been the original lead guitarist with Jethro Tull – whose new line-up appeared at the 1970 Festival – and played on their first LP until a personality clash with Ian Anderson saw him off. He later became a financial adviser, while saxophonist Jack Lancaster went on to play with many jazz fusion bands. Anderson recalls:

'That was one of my straightest days. We walked about a thousand yards through the dust to the stage. It was a great audience. We did our set and stayed for twenty minutes before we left. I got home to see myself on the nine o'clock news.'

The 1969 programme summed up the band well...

'Blodwyn Pig as a unit are not only unique – they are quite mad and admit it. Their ad-lib announcements, their pure delight in their performances, their unpredictability which also ensures a different and refreshing act at every appearance, puts them in a class of their own.'

EDGAR BROUGHTON BAND

Edgar Broughton had the crowd raving. His band provided the day's most memorable moments. They whipped up the crowd's excitement with their first number 'The Psychopath' to such an extent that during their next song a girl, completely naked, walked to the front of the stage and danced for a full five minutes before being led away by a security guard. Earlier, Edgar chanted his trademark 'Out, Demons, Out', and proved that no one need fear mass rioting from his crowd stirring methods after all. For a would-be revolutionary, Edgar's logic lacked in logic what it made up for in passion. To quote the programme,

> *'We're coming out of the underground to the other people. You know, there are bands that play for the underground, but we go out and tell people, "Look, there are people that know, that care, and want you to be as free as they are"... free meaning free thinking, free from hang-ups. Underground in its literal sense because of what it consists of – whether it's a press medium or a music medium, or just one voice speaking – has got a purpose, which is subverting what's above, and that's what we want to do.'*

The Broughton Band were the staple of free festivals like Phun City, and appear on the *Glastonbury Fayre* LP with an interminable 'Out, Demons, Out'. They recently reformed.

AYNSLEY DUNBAR RETALIATION
They blew a violent set, which was considerably heightened by the appearance of Anette Brox for a vocal duet with her husband Victor. Keyboard player Tommy Eyre had joined since their appearance at the previous year's festival. One of the first – and best – British blues boom combos.

MARSHA HUNT
Writhing, twisting Marsha Hunt, straight from *Hair*. Delicate readers are advised to skip the next few paragraphs, drawn from press reports of the time.

She wore a rather attractive set of leather knickers and a black sleeveless vest cut away slightly at the bottom. Her whole message was sex, plus a certain satirical glee. A big phallic microphone dangled loose between her legs, bumping up against her crutch, and was occasionally brought caressingly upwards, between expert-seeming fingertips, almost to the suck. Tremendous. Fantastic. Her excursions into satire consisted of sudden, smouldering looks fixed at random on a press man and held till his eyes averted. She was having fun. She sang 'Wild Thing' even. But everything, really, including 'Walk On Gilded Splinters', sounded like another encore of the same striptease show.

The pressmen slobbered at her brown, sexy feet. She's Negro and her hair stands out like a black halo in a seven-inch long freak-out from her skull. She is the prettiest golliwog in London.

Those were days before political correctness was even dreamed of!

Years later, Marsha herself explained the source of her attraction, under the headline, 'Knickers, that's how Marsha "beat" Dylan'.

'At the IOW, I got as much publicity as Bob Dylan, and we were dreadful. The band hadn't rehearsed and I was just out of hospital from having a cleft vocal chord so I didn't have any voice. On one of my numbers one of the musicians played the wrong song throughout, that's how appaling we were. But because I came out in black knickers and a black vest I got so much publicity. It was a joke.'

Marsha Hunt later had a love child by Mick Jagger. She has continued to record, and was a member of the National Theatre. She published her autobiography, *Real Life*, in 1986.

DISCO

Between bands, DJ Jeff Dexter – a long-haired blonde – played all the latest groovy sounds; the most popular records were the Great Awakening's 'Amazing Grace' – which re-emerged next year to become the Afton anthem – John Lennon's 'Give Peace A Chance', 'Honky Tonk Women' by the Stones, and 'Hare Krishna'.

It is not recorded whether the Bonzos performed their 'Harry Maynard' chant, or Viv Stanshall's heartfelt plea of a piss-take, 'Give Booze A Chance', to even up the balance.

Things get a bit hazy now. Certainly the Pretty Things played; in fact their set considerably overran. This led to some later groups either not performing at all – the oddly named Battered Ornaments, without leader Pete Brown, who they'd just sacked, but with future Womble Chris Spedding – or playing radically curtailed sets. Free were only on stage for fifteen minutes, although they made up for it in 1970 with perhaps the best gig of their young lives.

Co-incidentally my copy of the 1969 programme has both Blonde On Blonde and White Trash crossed out in purple ink. Marsha Hunt's remarks about her unrehearsed backing band would bare (sic) this out. On the other hand, one reliable witness claims that Liverpool Scene played a short set on Saturday, as well as opening on Sunday. After all this time, the exact running order is sometimes difficult to ascertain, which doesn't stop it being fun trying.

PRETTY THINGS

The Pretty Things played one of their least inspiring sets, with two drummers, which released Twink to clown around. Members of Fat Mattress joined them on stage, a combination described by one witness as like 'dumplings and lumpy gravy'. To add to the confusion, Dick Taylor is not listed in the Festival programme – though he appears in the accompanying photograph, helping lock Twink in a phone box – but definitely remembers joining the band after three numbers. He certainly took part in a very long version of the Byrds' song 'Why'.

Poet and *Private Eye* contributor Christopher Logue remembers giving a short reading – his copy of *New Numbers* shaking in his hand – at about eight o'clock, between the Pretty Things and Family.

FAMILY

Within minutes, vocalist Roger Chapman had smashed a tambourine to pieces and almost lassoed photographers with the microphone. Musically, they were a wall of sound, as Barry King recalls.

'I felt I could put my hands up and actually feel it. Great band, great performance.'

Chapman idiot danced, and the band's equipment was too knackered by their performance to allow an encore, so saxophonist Jim King – a sinister figure – played a solo piece to appease the crowd. Their entry in the Festival programme says everything, or perhaps nothing.

> *'We sometimes imagine ourselves to be a tree. Our roots are firmly set amongst us, the trunk resembles our progress and development and the branches are our directions. At the ends lie the fruits where they are to be taken by the people.'*

Chapman and guitarist John Whitney later founded Streetwalkers, before Chapman began a solo career which has since taken off in Germany, but nowhere else. Watching Family could be unexpectedly dangerous for those in the front row, into which Chapman would often fall, or throw the odd mike stand, in his simulation of an acid trip on stage! He always claimed afterwards that he could remember nothing of the performance.

It was now that Free did their three numbers, and were hustled off stage to make way for the Who, whose helicopter was approaching the site.

THE WHO

Potential anarchy always lurks at the heart of any outdoor event of this magnitude – which makes the Foulk's control throughout all the more commendable, and prefigured events of a year ahead.

Tragedy came closest when the Who nearly crash-landed onto the site. As their helicopter landed behind the stage on a 'H' marked out with wooden boards, one of the boards flew up into the rotor blade putting the 'copter out of action. The Who flew back to the mainland immediately after their act in another helicopter. 'We had wanted to land on the stage, but they wouldn't let us,' Townshend later commented.

Refugees from Woodstock, held two weeks earlier, the Who's set was so loud that large signs were erected in front of the stage, warning the audience to keep at least fifteen feet from the speakers. Townshend joked that the PA was built from Meccano, but it had a range of thirty miles, entertaining the prisoners in Parkhurst and the monks at Quarr, as well as many irate Island residents and, with 2,600 watts at their disposal, the citizens of Portsmouth as well.

Keith Moon had to have pain-killing injections in both legs in order to play after his recent accident in which he broke a foot bone. Daltrey's singing was stronger than usual, while visually he was a whirlwind. Townshend, in white boiler suit, was also in phenomenal form. He later described the Isle of Wight event as 'the most exhilarating pop experience I've ever been exposed to', and has been a frequent visitor to the Island ever since. Moon, Entwistle and Daltrey gave the audience an hour of electric rock at its most electrifying.

They opened with 'Heaven And Hell', 'I Can't Explain' and 'Fortune Teller', then Townshend played one of the best guitar solos in Who history on Mose Allison's 'Young Man Blues'. They performed the entire seventeen numbers from *Tommy*, which was interrupted by applause for 'Pinball Wizard'. 'Tommy, Can You Hear Me' echoing round the massive Festival site was really something. Then 'Summertime Blues' and 'My Generation', encoring finally with 'Shaking All Over', and perfunctory equipment bashing to conclude.

Having signed up months before for £450, manager Kit Lambert had phoned up the day before to say he wanted £5,000 instead. In the end, he accepted £1,000. A complete tape of their performance is in circulation. The Who returned for an even more successful – and lucrative – IOW appearance the following year. As Townshend later said,

'What was incredible about the Isle of Wight thing was that the Who were totally and completely in control.'

FAT MATTRESS

They had a tough time following the Who. It was their first British performance. It was also a farce. Visually, they were nothing – no charisma, no focal point. The lead singer looked like an even more ridiculous parody of Christopher Logue than Christopher Logue did.

None of the instruments escaped from the formless, pointless noise that earned them a whisper of applause and no encore. Their regular attempts at frenzy were as ineffectual as their less frequent tries for delicacy.

Noel Redding, bassist with the Jimi Hendrix Experience, played lead guitar; the rest of the musicians were drawn from his previous band, The Loving Kind. Redding was the only member of the original three-piece Experience not to play with Hendrix in the 1970 Afton Festival. Of the 1969 event, he recalled...

> '...a mad party from the time we boarded the ferry. The weather was great and the gig was good. We went on at midnight and left at dawn to drive to our gig in Redcar, North Riding.'

After Fat Mattress's rapid and inevitable demise, Redding suffered from a drug related decline, although he is now playing in bar bands in Ireland. His advise to young musicians is, 'Go to law school, learn accounting, and get a gun.'

JOE COCKER AND THE GREASE BAND

Pete Townshend had already given Joe Cocker a plug in his own set. 'There's a change taken place and he's gonna be very, very exciting to you all.' Both were Woodstock survivors, and stars of the forthcoming film. Next year's IOW line-up was almost a carbon copy – and it too became a free festival through force of numbers – with Richie Havens, Joan Baez, would add Ten Years After, Sly And The Family Stone, John Sebastian and Jimi Hendrix, all relocating from Woodstock Nation to Freshwater Bay.

While the Grease Band swung beautifully and sounded great after the shambles of the Pretty Things and the low interest of Fat Mattress, Joe himself did not quite make contact with the audience. He sang well, but soul seemed a trifle out of place in this context, and his stage movements irritated some while hypnotising others. Never was there a better player of the invisible guitar.

One of the finest soul singers of all time, backed by a Grease Band led by keyboard player Chris Stainton, the Festival programme outlined Cocker's rise to fame:

> *'The gas fitter from Sheffield who sang 'With A Little Help From My Friends'. We saw him first at last year's Windsor Festival with the Grease Band, when he did a beautiful version of 'I Shall Be Released'. He generates the same kind of dynamism, unseen in a singer, since the early days of the Rolling Stones. Britain's answer to Blind Sam McVitie started singing at sixteen and admits to a big Ray Charles influence. He stopped for a while and took a job with W.H. Smith before joining the Grease Band for his first record, 'Marjorine'.'*

Cocker subsequently joined Mad Dogs And Englishmen, stage managed by Leon Russell – a feature film was made of them falling apart on the road – and went into something of a decline, though he is still performing and recording. When 'With A Little Help From My Friends' again reached No. 1 as performed by Wet, Wet, Wet he performed it with them for the Prince's Trust concert. Still a legend.

MOODY BLUES

The concerts rolled on into early Sunday morning. Their performance really stood out, particularly a spine-tingling 'Nights In White Satin'. The coloured lighting effects were as beautiful as the music, and they even played an encore, the first in their history.

After a vast wave of applause and cheering which sounded like a Nuremberg rally, the Moodies said, 'We have waited five years to hear that.' Despite problems with their Mellotron which distorted slightly and took the edge off their impact, the Moodies settled down to a full sounding programme which also included 'Dr Livingstone I Presume' and 'Never Comes The Day'.

Ignoring their early hit 'Go Now', they instead performed songs from their *Days Of Future Past* LP, a chronicle of one day from morning to night, to conclude Saturday's rich menu of entertainment. People left the arena, went to sleep outside the gate and were therefore in the queue for Sunday's show, all through the night and all Sunday morning.

6

Sunday 31 August, 1969

Dylan day started early. The flow of arrivals into the seething twenty acre arena seemed endless. Dylan himself must have felt the tension in his farmhouse at Bembridge, five miles to the east. Throughout the day, a stream of pilgrims continued to arrive, tired and leg-weary. Some were resting on the pavement, others in the roadside. After a morning of film shows and audience talent contests, the Liverpool Scene got things underway at midday. As each act appeared, the audience swelled both in number and in excited anticipation of Dylan's 'second coming'. According to *Isle Of Wight Rock*, Gypsy again prefaced proceedings, this time with a bugle player. Good morning campers!

LIVERPOOL SCENE
First on were the Liverpool Scene with their mixture of pop and poetry. Overweight, bearded Liverpool poet Adrian Henri bounded about the stage with remarkable energy. 'Let's see if we can wake up Bob Dylan from here,' he yelled. And he went into a number about an American rock 'n' roll group who died when a soda fountain exploded in New York, drowning 200 people in soda ice-cream.

This was a cross-cultural happening. As the programme summed it up,

'The Liverpool Scene has come a long way from the loose collection of poets and musicians who performed their stuff to students in duffle-coats and jeans holding pints in the bar under the Everyman Theatre, Liverpool, in the winter of 1966–67. John Peel started reading their work on Perfumed Garden and a booking at London's UFO followed almost immediately. Since then Roger McGough, Brian Patten, Mike Hart and others have gone their separate ways and the line-up, still dominated by the immense, baggy figure of Adrian Henri, has settled down to its present five.'

Part of their set was captured by the Pathe News cameras, and shown in cinemas across the country. Andy Roberts remembers that their kit consisted of a Selmer thirty watt amp, and home-made bass amp and drums. Hardly the Grateful Dead, but they made a pleasant racket.

Adrian Henri has since slimmed down, and is now a painter. With McGough and Patten he defined a whole school of sixties poetry. Roberts formed Plainsong with Ian Matthews, while bassist Percy Jones was a founder member of jazz–rock group Brand X.

THIRD EAR BAND

Like the Liverpool Scene, veterans of the UFO, where the theft of their amplification left them to forge an identity as an acoustic group. Their free-form improvisations using tablas, cello, violin and oboe in weird configurations later graced Polanski's *Macbeth*. Their use of drone-like figures and extended compositions linked them to the experimental work of Terry Riley, and prefigured the ambient music of the 1980s. They were also very much of their time, as the programme note indicates.

'The music is the music of the Druids, released from the unconscious by the alchemical process, orgasmic in its otherness, religious in its oneness, communicating beauty and

magic via abstract sounds whilst playing without ego enables the musicians to reach a trance-like state, a "high" in which the music produces itself. Each piece is as alike or unalike as blades of grass or clouds.'

When I first saw them, they spent five minutes tuning up, then repeated this eight times, and I gradually realised that they were playing for real! At the 1990 Festival, I asked tabla player Glen Sweeney what had happened to them meanwhile, and his eyes rotated in the massive shaved dome of his head as he explained that he had had to 'go away for a while'.

Cellist Paul Buckminster left the band to become a respected arranger; he was responsible for the strings on Carly Simon's hit single 'You're So Vain'.

INDO-JAZZ FUSIONS

It was 3 pm. Like the Third Ear Band, Indo-Jazz Fusions served up a rhythmic distillation of eastern and western musical ideas, prefiguring current interest in 'world music'. A great relief after a surfeit of heavy rock the previous night.

The sun came out on Sunday afternoon and listening to the Third Ear Band and then to the more substantial Indo-Jazz Fusions was like the film *Jazz On A Summer's Day*. But by the time Tom Paxton came on, it had gone cold and windy again and people seemed none too happy.

A more positive witness – Rikki Farr – described the day as cloudy but not cold – perfect festival weather. What followed was a day of folk music, alternating English denizens of the Soho coffee cellar scene, and their American counterparts, singer–songwriters who had established their reputations in Greenwich Village, the very people who Dylan kissed off in 'Positively Fourth Street', when he turned his back on folk music for electric rock, Beatle boots and dark shades.

GARY FARR

Gary Farr, Rikki's brother, proved to be a pleasing singer and songwriter in the folk-rock style, with 'Good Morning Sun' and a country blues tinged 'The Vicar And The Pope' – the best songs in his set. He was subtly backed by members of Mighty Baby, formerly mod group the Action with the deranged addition of lead guitarist supreme Martin Stone, who had just quit Savoy Brown after instigating the first drugs bust in Devon.

'Gary lives in solitude in a quiet country cottage, enjoying simplicity in all things. He played for five years with the T. Bones before writing and performing his own work; his songs are personal and sincerely felt.'
Programme note

Farr sadly died in Los Angeles in August 1994.

TOM PAXTON

Next came American singer-songwriter Tom Paxton, who received one of the biggest ovations of the Festival. This was quite unexpected, but honestly deserved.

Paxton was described by poet Christopher Logue as 'a short, cherubic West-Coaster who dresses like a German submariner from the First World War'. He began nervously and rather sadly: on the Saturday, he had appeared in the press arena wearing a piece of paper saying 'Tom Paxton' on his lapel. But after some old favourites – 'Where I'm Bound', 'Ramblin' Boy', 'Last Thing On My Mind' – he warmed up and got a very warm reception indeed. As an encore, he did a biting, brilliant 'Vietnam Pot-Luck Blues'. This caused a storm. Paxton had humanised the audience. He made them feel cared for.

He had to do another encore, 'Forest Lawn', a comment on the American way of dying. After this, there was a standing ovation that lasted longer than those accorded the Who. Back a third time? No, he really couldn't because, it was explained (quite untruthfully) that he had to fly back at once to a US concert commitment. In fact, he spent the rest of the afternoon drinking in the press bar and then came into the press arena to see Dylan's performance.

Even after being told that he was emphatically not coming back on stage, the audience stayed on their feet, roaring, 'We want Tom', then fell into a chant of 'Paxton, Paxton, Paxton', which lasted fully four minutes. It was, because so unexpected, overwhelming. And when Paxton did, after all this, come back, he came to the microphone and said, 'Thank you, thank you. You've made me happier than I've ever been in my whole life.'

Real tears came to peoples' eyes. It was fantastic. Tom Paxton continues to tour and to release LPs, though he is Radio 2 material now. He is also a very successful songwriter for children; like all those of talent rather than pretension, his work has lasted the process of time, but he will never again be a legend!

PENTANGLE

Pentangle had a somewhat tougher time than Paxton. Very much a listening band, and predating Fairport in the combination of folk purity and jazz inflections. Both Bert Jansch and John Renbourne were fine acoustic guitarists dominating the Soho scene of the mid-sixties. Their set was spoiled by several incidents. Low flying aircraft drowned out their music at one point, a small fire on the arena perimeter caused a loss of interest and to cap it all the Rolling Stones chose to make their entry in the middle of the murder ballad 'Bruton Town'. However, they cut through with 'Pentangling', which included one of Danny Thompson's inimitable double bass solos.

A less favourable account remembers...

> '...an uninteresting and at times incompetent performance, full of dreary sensitiveness and signifying little. Perhaps their music was too intimate and low key for such a massive and edgy crowd to appreciate. Or perhaps it really was dire!'

Pentangle recently reformed, in a low key kind of way. Danny Thompson has gone on to play with his namesake Richard, and to become a stalwart of the 'world music' scene. His musical lineage is long and distinguished, from Tim Buckley to Ketama.

JULIE FELIX

Then came American folk singer and television show hostess, Julie Felix who sang sweetly on a selection that included 'I Want To Be Alone' by Soho legend Jackson C. Frank, 'Laughing Len', Cohen's 'Bird On A Wire', and her own 'On A Windy Morning'. She also sang the first Dylan songs of the day, 'Chimes Of Freedom' and 'Masters Of War', at the audience's request. This brought her a big round of cheers and applause.

She was overcome by her reception. 'This is really wonderful. You're beautiful,' she smiled. In the heat of the moment, she could think of nothing to sing for her encore. 'We want 'The Zoo',' the crowd chanted. She sang it.

At this point there was a chilling foretaste of next year's hippie anarchy. Sebastian Jorgensen, who had been working on *Homosexual Oz*, leapt onto the stage and tried to strum a guitar in time. 'He's tripping,' Richard Neville's girl friend told him. 'He's off the planet.' Dylan was getting nearer and the crowd's excitement was stretched almost to breaking point.

RICHIE HAVENS

With dusk settling in on the vast open air arena, Richie Havens, a truly dynamic singer, came on. 'His voice is curdled molasses,' observed Richard Neville from side stage. Wearing a white robe, decorated with paths of blue and yellow beads, Havens set a clear, strong rhythm going and sang plain, almost single word lyrics to it. Havens had arrived from the States early on Sunday morning, and was the last attraction before Dylan and the Band.

One of the few black performers in the Festival, Havens had been born in a Brooklyn ghetto. At seventeen, he moved to Greenwich Village where he sang in coffee houses like the Gaslight and the Cafe Wha, influenced by fellow singers like Dino Valenti and, of course, Dylan.

Accompanied by Paul Williams on guitar and conga player Danielle Benzebulon, Havens worked out beautifully on 'Maggie's Farm', and his own soulful arrangement of 'Strawberry Fields Forever', with the chorus of 'Hey Jude' thrown in, and won huge appreciation for his intense, powerful singing of his own songs, 'Freedom' and 'Run Shaker Life', if not for his between song pronouncements. 'My guitar IS,' he said.

'My guitar has come a long way in the last twenty-four hours. It has probably touched every element known to man. It has been on the earth. It has been on the water...'

At least one witness wished it had caught on fire!

His music, though, was 'exciting, assured, powerful, coherent' and he got two encores. The Grossman stable had almost justified its collective top billing. The programme note aptly claimed:

> *'Havens is a pure example of the ecstatic singer, open to love and to emotion and on fire with a glorious view of the future.'*

In a colder age, he was last heard of singing advertising jingles. When he left the stage, at 8.19 pm, daylight was already gone. Christopher Logue caught the scene beautifully. There was...

> *'...a sunset glorious enough to delight Turner. One of those long, endless skies streaked with lines of pink cloud, emerald light behind them, the on-coming darkness pouring through it, changing the upper greens to blue, to cobalt, to indigo, and the helicopters fluttering their red and amber guide lights overhead. It was as if Apollo had noticed us and, in passing, given the show a nod.'*

The pilgrims waited, listening to records from the stage. The new Apple single, 'Hare Krishna', echoed across the Bay and over the Solent. The air was thick with the scent of hamburgers and joss-sticks. Trees lining the arena, lit by nearby lamps, were filled with penniless hippies taking a free view. Excitement in the packed arena reached an all-time high as the long wait went on.

International Times prefigured *Hello* magazine.

> *'Oh yes, and all the stars were there; some Rolling Stones, some Beatles, Françoise Hardy, lovely in leather, Jane Fonda with Vadim and everyone, my dear.'*

After Havens there was over an hour's pause during which the audience waited doggedly, a little cynically and the 2,000 people in the press arena, meant to hold 300, began pushing and shoving and taking more photographs of the famous (Peter Wyngarde, Terence Stamp, even Cilla Black!). There was little love and gentleness emanating from this bearpit, not least when the seating was rearranged to allow 'Mr Grossman's Party', which numbered around seventy, to grab all the best places. When Dylan eventually took the stage, a few missiles were thrown not, as was alleged, at him, but at photographers and others blocking the view.

Curtains were draped across the stage, posh in royal blue. Thick, proletarian microphones, one per instrument, were exchanged for elegant, design-award microphones in large numbers, grouped tastefully around a cleaner, more ethereally lit stage. By now the atmosphere was becoming electric as the audience approached its expected 200,000. Furious at the delay, Dylan kept sending his road manager Al Aronowitz out to find out what was going wrong.

'What the fuck's wrong with the fuckin' sound system!' he shouted at the hapless journalist. 'What's takin' so fuckin' long?!?' After Al had come back a third time, feeling rather like the man sent to hurl Excalibur into the lake, Dylan screamed, 'I want the band on NOW! RIGHT NOW!'

THE BAND

Finally, it happened, the curtain drew back, the lights flashed down. At 10.21 pm, on stage walked the Band – but minus Dylan. The Band was a complete knock-out in its own right. A fantastic driving sound with beautiful tightness and great rocking drums from Levon Helm. They looked so pleased to be playing, and their sound was intoxicating. So infectious was the humour and dignified passion of the group's set that calls for Dylan subsided until almost the end of their set.

They immediately swung into a jubilant 'We Can Talk'. Their sound was very clear, warm and heavy without being crushing, and tempered with a strong country feel. At times, with the piano and organ line-up, they were reminiscent of Procol Harum. Most of their numbers were taken from their first album. Next came 'Long Black Veil' and a rare live version of 'To Kingdom Come', with Robertson hoarsely yelling vocals out with all the others.

Drummer Levon Helm switched to his 1930s mandolin for a couple of straight country songs, 'Ain't No More Cane' and 'Don't Ya Tell

Henry'. 'Hope country music goes down alright in the Isle o' Wight,' Robertson commented.

Next came 'Chest Fever', 'I Shall Be Released' and their hit single 'The Weight'. The Band finished their set with a frantic, country-rock version of the Four Tops' 'Loving You (Made My Life Sweeter Than Ever)'.

One journalist present noted that they were an amplified version of old stories told round a camp fire, while for Nic Cohn,

> *'Their harmonies half country, half gospel and the beat good hard rock, they made the endless succession of English bands that had gone before seem like so much Mickey Mouse.'*

There were outstanding performances by Rick Danko on bass who had a fast energetic style, his right hand slapping the strings as if they were red hot, and by Robbie Robertson on guitar who has absorbed the heavy rock sound, mixed it with country and gives it back with short, succinct, imaginative and beautiful seering solos, sometimes as mellow as a harpsichord, sometimes as sharp as cactus blades.

The audience were thrown when the Band abruptly turned and left the stage upon completion of their act in normal American style. By the time they realised what was happening it was too late to applaud or cheer for more. They had played for forty-five minutes.

> *'I suppose a lot of people are going to try to call us Bob Dylan's band, but even he doesn't call us that,' says Robertson. 'The only name that we do have is the name of our neighbours, friends and people who know us call us. They call us the band.'*
> Programme note

The Band never quite realised their massive potential, and broke up in 1978, an event commemorated in Martin Scorsese's film – and multi-album set – *The Last Waltz*. Their influence can be judged by those who turned up to mourn their passing, Dylan himself of course, and Van Morrison, Neil Young, even Neil Diamond. The Band's music was a healing force in a post-hippie world, a deep search for roots and commitment matched by the Grateful Dead and Fairport, among other luminaries.

Keyboard player Richard Manuel, a singer and songwriter whose haunting melancholy was matched only by Nick Drake, David Accles and Tim Buckley – all too lost in the shuffle of time – later committed suicide following a concert by the reformed Band, after a long history of drug and drink abuse.

Robertson refused to join any such reunion, acted in the film *Carney* and has worked on many film soundtracks. He recently released two solo LPs, and a concept work which celebrated his own roots in the Indian nation, a heritage shared with Jimi Hendrix and Johnny Cash.

Another pause. The return of Rikki Farr.

> *'People – do you want the sound to be perfect?'*
> *'Yeah.'*
> *'Then cool it, people. You've waited three days. Be cool and wait another five minutes and you'll have the sound a hundred per cent perfect. In fact you'll have it two hundred per cent perfect.'*

Finally, just prior to 11 pm there were signs of activity. The stage was lit. The standard Dylan stool, reputedly loaned by the local folk club based at the nearby Sloop Inn stood in place...

BOB DYLAN

At 11.08 pm, Dylan strolled on stage to the largest live audience even he had ever faced in his life. 'You sure look big out there,' he said. Under the spotlight, Dylan wore a loose fitting all-white suit, with short hair and a scrubby beard: the crowd greeted him with an ecstatic roar.

> *'The only performer who could afford not to wear flared, sexy trousers, dressed all in white, with a yellow shirt, perfect. Like a worrying but ecstatic dream.'*

He reinterpreted much earlier work in the light of *Nashville Skyline*. He smiled like Bugs Bunny, and repeated, in a shy voice, 'Great to be here, really great.' Dylan tried, by a fluttering, Orbison-like lyric eloquence, to take every nuance of bitterness and cynicism out of his songs. He has constantly re-interpreted himself, and this was the apocalypse revisited as a back porch, family singalong.

Dylan began with 'She Belongs To Me' with which he also opened the acoustic half of his 1966 tour with the Hawks. This time round the performance was smoother, less drawn out, and Dylan glided smoothly through the lyric. Robertson punctuated the song with bluesey, laid back guitar.

Dylan looked and sounded nervous, backing away from the microphone after each song, seeking comfort from a little backchat with the Band, and rolling through his repertoire as if he'd just rewritten the tunes and meddled with the words. The Band backed him brilliantly, playing as if Dylan was just part of the group. He used the country music form of 'one more time' to inform them when he wanted a number to end.

'I Threw It All Away' was beautiful, and taken very slowly. '*Love is all there is, it makes the world go 'round*', he sang, and the audience believed his every word. 'Maggie's Farm' had earlier been performed as a folk blues by Richie Havens. Dylan rocked it up and shouted the crushing lyrics while the Band echoed 'no more' again and again, thrusting their faces towards the barrage of mikes, exchanging grins.

The Band now left the stage, as Dylan launched into a solo set with the traditional Scottish folk-song 'Wild Mountain Thyme', sung with great affection, and featuring some lovely acoustic guitar work. 'It Ain't Me Babe' followed, which wasn't suited to his new vocal phrasing and voice, and the tempo seemed a little stilted. The song was too bitter and cutting to be resurrected in his latest image. 'To Ramona' was closer to the recorded version, though it lacked the poignancy of the song as it appeared on *Another Side*.

Claps, shrieks, cheers, whistles greeted the first bars of 'Mr Tambourine Man'. Dylan used his harmonica for the only time that night – 'two brief puffs of it'. More than one of the audience felt at this point that 'a loving wistfulness pervaded the atmosphere and we all felt here is Bob Dylan, in front of us, flesh and blood, really here.

As the Band returned, Dylan's strangely expressive eyes were checking out that all was going well. His smile, and the Band's, confirmed that it was. They launched into 'I Dreamed I Saw St Augustine', and Robertson played a nice guitar solo in the middle. Dylan himself was now in the habit of lifting his guitar to straddle his chest, like a rifle, in the middle of each song, and the effect was strangely menacing. Faces were still alight when he sang 'Lay Lady Lay'.

Dylan rocked his way through 'Highway 61 Revisited'. Grins and smiles and laughs of delight, as the Band provided a sensationally rocking country backdrop, loudly yelling, *Down on Highway Sixty One'*. They roared out the backing vocals like wild dogs, and even threw in a Saturday morning Granada organ solo which lay nicely behind the pounding cowboy rock. It was all too much and Dylan at last seemed to be relaxing into his performance.

Dylan set 'One Too Many Mornings', cataclysmic in the 1966 version, a vision of apocalypse rather than lost love, to the beat of 'It Takes A Lot To Laugh, It Takes A Train To Cry'. The most telling moment was during the line, *'Everything I'm a saying, you can say it just as good'*, during which he raised his hand to the crowd. It seemed to suggest a warning that the myths pushed out about him through the media over the past couple of weeks were not to be believed, that he was nothing special.

The Band's arrangement of 'I Pity The Poor Immigrant' – another song of modesty and restraint – was haunting, with Garth Hudson particularly effective on accordion. Dylan's greatest single, 'Like A Rolling Stone', was given a jerky vocal treatment, and worked brilliantly, propelled along on a groove half way between Stax and Phil Spector, with Levon Holm's locomotive drumming. The Band yelled out 'How does it feel', while Dylan used the additional device of adding the word 'girl' in judicious places: *'You mustn't let other people get their kicks for you, girl'*.

'I'll Be Your Baby Tonight' followed and was given a less mellow treatment than the single, with considerable beat. The charm remained even for a bubbly version of 'Mighty Quinn', graced by one of Robertson's most coruscating guitar solos of the night. 'This is a song that was a big hit in England for Manfred Mann. A great group, great group,' said Bob.

He went off and was called back. But he didn't return for a couple of minutes. Someone near me said, in all seriousness, 'Dylan's too big to do an encore, man.' He wasn't, and launched into his first new song of the evening, 'Minstrel Boy', a gospel-tinged number.

The *Oz* cartoonist and poster artist Martin Sharp was side stage – he had produced one of the most famous images of Dylan, wreathed in bubbles. At this point he flicked a two shilling piece near Dylan, as he sang, *'Please throw a coin to the poor minstrel boy'*. It can be clearly heard on a bootleg recording of the set. A 'zen moment'.

Dylan finished with 'Rainy Day Woman Nos 12 & 35', though it lacked the stoned atmosphere of the *Blonde On Blonde* original. Dylan sang it straight, as a country rock tune. And that was that, no superstar jams, no four-hour sets, no blinding revelations. Dylan left the stage obviously exhausted; seemingly stiff and drained as Al Aronowitz relieved him of his guitar.

Levon Helm:

'I would've like to have gotten carried away... and Bob had an extra list of songs with eight or ten different titles with question marks by them, that we would've went ahead and done, had it seemed like the thing to do. But it seemed like everybody was a bit tired and the Festival was three days old by then and so, if everybody else is ready to go home, let's go.'

At least no one had shouted out 'Judas'. *Rolling Stone* foamed at the mouth.

'It was an exquisite con. It was brilliant. It was the best thing that's happened on a British stage since the 1966 concerts by the same untouchable, charismatic man. The crowd, knowing perfectly well that there was no practical point in doing so,

stood and shouted for more for at least twenty solid minutes.
Our Father which art back in thy villa with thy £35,000 already,
forgive thyself thy trespass against us.'

'I think I prefer the new Dylan you know,' someone said on the way out as he passed a portable record player playing 'Masters Of War'.

'Thank you, thank you, great!' And Dylan was gone.

The strange and very rapid disappearance of Dylan should really have been anticipated, but it nevertheless left all nine acres of listeners gaping in amazement at the sudden end. Chants began, pleas of 'More' rang out in great volumes. Disturbed, the crowd went up on its feet, but Rikki Farr returned to the stage and said in his now tired voice,

'He's gone... he's gone. He came here to do what he had to do,
he did it for you and now he's gone. Really, there is no more...'

And so, tent pegs were pulled out of the ground, sleeping bags rolled up and packs packed. Like lava flowing down the sides of a smouldering volcano, the people poured out between the hundreds of bonfires and started for the long series of queues that lay between them and home.

John Lennon had arrived early and stayed for most of Saturday and Sunday, displaying great enthusiasm for the event. With other celebrities, he had taken his seat just before Dylan's spot and made a hasty escape just before he did his encore. For Lennon's biographer, Ray Coleman,

'Dylan radiates an almost mystical warmth. If anyone went
away from this frail giant's concert wondering what all the
fuss was about, it's probably no good trying to explain.'

This did not capture the sense of anti-climax that many felt after Dylan's performance. Barry Miles, who later wrote the definitive study of Dylan's friend and fellow poet Allen Ginsurg, probably came closest to explaining what had gone wrong.

'Even if Dylan had levitated, produced stigmata and electric bolts from his fingertips, it would have been a let down. The popular press had elevated him to a messianic position with phony interviews, non-event news and general purpose pin-up space fillers.

'It was obvious that Dylan wanted to be regarded not as a figure-head, saint, saviour or leader, but as a performer. His emphasis on the words of 'It Ain't Me Babe', together with searching looks into the audience, affirmed this.'

The concert was part of Dylan's deliberate policy of escaping his messiah role, of deconstructing the expectations he had – at times deliberately – fostered. The subsequent double LP *Self Portrait* was a deliberate act of artistic suicide, and contained performances of songs from the Isle of Wight Festival: 'Like A Rolling Stone', 'She Belongs To Me', 'The Mighty Quinn' and 'Minstrel Boy'.

Dylan himself went straight off the site back to Forelands, where there was a small gathering. He left the Island the next day, by hovercraft, and then by private helicopter to Lennon's home, Tittenhurst Park, where he played piano on a rough mix of 'Cold Turkey'. On Tuesday, he boarded a flight back to New York, seen off by George and Patti Harrison. Back in the States, he admitted to having had 'a rather grand time', but stated that he had no desire to return. 'They make too much of singers there. Singers are front page news.'

Fleet Street was unimpressed. The *Daily Sketch* described Dylan's reception as 'cool compared with the enthusiasm for the pop groups who appeared earlier'. Some of the press people walked out mid-performance (while hundreds were frantically trying to break into the arena, and breaking bones in the process).

There was an amazing atmosphere throughout the Dylan-Band performance; one witness reports arriving half way through, and being struck by the crowd's extraordinary silence, as if in a trance.

'Everybody was taken out of their heads, out of their bodies and out of the whole Dig This Heavy Sound movie. They

*realised that excessive cheering would not only break the spell
but also bug Dylan more than the flashing photographers.'*

Afterwards, the cheering was ecstatic and continued for an infinity.
Everyone in the huge crowd was smiling, a fact totally beyond the grasp
of the press, for whom it was inconceivable that people, including
Dylan himself, should have been made happy by what had just taken
place.

Of course, press hostility could date back to the Saturday, when
Rikki Farr had announced from the stage,

'You people from the Sketch *and* Mirror *and* People, *you should
be ashamed of yourselves; you write a lot of shit.'*

Not the most diplomatic of comments, even if true! No one who
attended would ever forget Woodside Bay, the huge searchlights from
the lighting rig shining out like prison towers in some World War II
movie, as Farr read frantic messages from people who had lost friends,
money, possessions or their minds! To match this, even shared
discomfort enhanced the overall feeling of community, of being part of
a larger being. Here was the opportunity of living one's alternative
lifestyle, free from police, straight neighbours or any authoritarian
moral restrictions, at least for a few days.

Rikki Farr became part priest, part parish pump, as he read an
agony column of messages over the mike. Someone had lost his
diabetic tablets. Someone's husband had been lost, and would Farr
speak the message loudly since the husband was hard of hearing.
Someone was broke and hungry and needed bread from a friend,
bread of both kinds, someone's black and tan spaniel had disappeared
and if anyone saw it the dog's name was Junkie, would Carol meet Joe
at the chip van at the back of the arena...

Richard Neville remembers British Rail being not up to the return
trip.

*'The station was a refugee camp, with everyone cold, wet,
hungry and stupified.'*

He met Sam Hutt, a young doctor later to reinvent himself as country and western singing star Hank Wangford. Dr Hutt's medical kit included a large bottle of green tincture of cannabis, available for prescription, which aided his journey home.

Within weeks, a video tape filmed by Jim Haynes of Dylan, the Who and other acts performing at the Festival was shown at the Arts Lab in Drury Lane. Wider exposure was given to the woman – naked apart from love beads, a wispy scarf and glasses – who was passed over a sea of heads into the media enclosure. Her photograph became a full-page ad – for the rock group Free – in *Oz* magazine, and its editor believes that another Australian media mogul, Rupert Murdoch, took this idea and turned it into the Page Three Girl in the *Sun* a few years later.

What really endured, however, could not be captured on film or in newsprint. Many people went to see Dylan, but came away with new friends and lasting relationships. The pop festival had replaced the communal aspect of large demonstrations like Aldermaston, with the same feelings of friendship, comradeship, and mutual respect. Even after the music finished, the nights were relaxed and beautiful, people promenading, meeting, talking, home-made music playing and flickering camp fires outside the tents and shacks of the shanty town.

There were treehouses, ingeniously erected in the woods surrounding the hundred acre arena, fields full of tents, the appealing honesty of the hippies who could leave their possessions unguarded knowing nobody would dream of stealing anything.

Those were happier, easier times. Hippies who took tickets to Ryde and found at the end of the weekend they had no money left were able to draw national assistance – especially supplied – to get them home. The Festival organisers also hoped to make a small profit. Said spokesman Peter Harrigan,

'We should make something in the region of £10,000 – which will be ploughed back into the organisation of the next festival.'

Dylan had received his fee in full before appearing, allegedly £35,000, working out at about £530 a minute. And £17 promptly went in Dylan's pre-act drinks bill for himself and his Beatles backstage admirers. As *Record Mirror* put it:

> *'Many a night of live, a moment of freak and an hour of good music had been shared at the biggest, most elaborate festival in history. Dylan had returned but maintained his mystic aura and once again a generation proved itself worthy of its ideals. A big hand for Fiery Creations' magnificent gesture and another for those countless thousands who sank the IOW not with a bang but with a respectful note of thanks.'*
>
> *'Thank you Dylan for coming, thank you organisers for organising, thank you the players for playing and, most of all, thank you all the people for your peace and behaviour.'*
> 1970 Festival prospectus

A little ironic, in view of the events that were to unfold in 1970.

7

Planning for the most
spectacular festival ever

In January 1970, an official prospectus was sent to interested parties, prefaced with a superb Dave Roe graphic on tissue paper. The proposed venue for the Third Isle of Wight Festival of Music was again Woodside Bay. Fiery Creations intended to 'present the world with the largest and most spectacular Festival ever', featuring 'the best available progressive music in the world'. In addition, 'a full ninety piece symphony orchestra will be featured, not only to accompany some of the acts, but also able to give their own performance of music from *2001: A Space Odyssey*'. The music would be spread over three days, reflecting the wide range of contemporary pop. Friday's entertainment would cover a broad range of rock music, Saturday would cater for heavy, 'underground' music, and Sunday would represent folk and folk-rock.

The range and sophistication of what was planned seems a precursor of the kind of stadium rock which is now a multi-million pound industry. Music would run for fourteen hours a day, and events on stage would be broadcast in colour on a forty by thirty foot video screen; the proposed system to utilise four camera crews. Shorter films would be screened between acts, and for the two days preceding the festival.

'Every assurance is given that the IOW Festival will offer better value for money than any other festival.' This claim was certainly fulfilled, though it still proved insufficient for some. The techniques of putting together such an intricate operation read like something out of a 1980s management manual:

> 'In the cause of efficiency and professionalism, the organisation is divided into twelve major departments, each handling a specific aspect of the Festival, headed by twelve key men and women who have all been selected for their ability to organise and their knowledge and expertise in the work they are doing. Each and every one of them is thoroughly capable and reliable, they are all answerable only to the directors of the Company.
>
> 'All of the department heads have an able team working under them. In some cases the departments are sub-divided into as many as ten smaller departments. Departments are all in some way connected with one another and this requires close liaison. To ensure the smooth running of the organisation, efficient systems are in operation.'

This business efficiency was, however, a means to an end, not merely its own rationale, as has happened to many once-vibrant organisations in the 1990s. There was a sense of ambition – towards building a community, not just an audience – which a more cynical age would find laughable, although the same aims have been successfully pursued at the annual Glastonbury Festival, very much the heir of the Isle of Wight events.

> 'By integrating multi-media activities with music and films, and with extensive audience participation, the event as a whole will run smoothly as a five-day happening and not just a series of acts going on and off stage. There is an open invitation extended to all people who have something to do or something to say. The opportunities for people to "do their own thing" before a large, discriminating audience, are rare.'

Little did the organisers know how literally this would come to pass!

The stage itself was to be designed and built on the lines of a World's Fair exhibition stand, with facilities for a thousand journalists, and a special area – like Ascot's Royal Enclosure – for a thousand celebrities and special guests. Who said that the sixties broke down the class barriers; it simply erected new ones. Plans were also underway to include a heliport on stage.

All 'artistes' were to have their own tent or caravan for changing and rest purposes. Private catering facilities with a waiter service and private toilet facilities were also provided, as was a tent with tuning up amplifiers, an artistes' bar and telephone facilities. A backstage speaker system to cue artistes on stage would also be in operation.

Catering for the masses was to be supplied by one company, working under the stringent control of Fiery Creations, to ensure reasonable prices, quality and quantity. This indeed proved to be the case, even though the site incorporated a small city, with a hundred shops in the main arena and thirty more in the camping area. It was no wonder that some of the leading spirits in Fiery Creations went on to plan that cathedral to mass shopping, Milton Keynes, and align it on the midsummer sunrise, just like Stonehenge!

The arena was to be patrolled by 250 uniformed security guards to 'ensure the well-being of all persons attending the Festival'. These guards would not be seen by the vast majority as they were to be posted between the two perimeter walls. Little did they know.

The 1970 event was to be at the cutting edge of acoustic technology. WEM had designed a special sound system, with...

'...forty hundred-watt output valved amplifiers linked in series, powered back to a twenty-five channel mixer, reduced down to three five-channel audio master mixer controls capable of giving echo, reverb, compression, and all known studio sound oscillations.

'Sound lines will run from the audiomaster to sixty four by twelve inch column, mid-range speakers, linked on a cross-over network to ten horn tweeters for high range spread and ten bass woofer cabinets for low range spread.

'There will be thirty-six microphones of low impedance and high impedance, plus condenser microphones with power packs, allowing the balance of sound from electric to acoustic

instruments to maintain a stabilised quality. There will also be foldback (cue) speakers on stage to assist artistes in their performance. All equipment is microphoned on stage and fed into the mixer unit, making sure of perfect balance at all times.

'Lighting will encompass two towers with "Lime" operators and follow spots. On stage, there will be in the region of 120 Kw lighting units to give all required lighting effects.'

Quite how all this technology could be paid for if there was no ticket admission charged was something the adherents of a free festival never got round to explaining. Ticket sales were to be distributed throughout the UK via about a thousand record shops and ticket agencies, and contact made with shops in all major European cities, and many in America and Canada. Over the weekend, tickets would be easily available to all, as the main arena could be enlarged to accommodate an unlimited number of music fans. And that, when Afton Down was still a quiet and remote hillside, little knowing what history had planned.

The 1970 Prospectus concludes with a short description of the Isle of Wight...

'...situated to the south of Portsmouth, Southampton and Bournemouth. It is separated from the mainland by the famous yachting haven, the Solent. It is about seventy miles south of London, and is known to have the warmest climate in the British Isles.

'Twenty-three miles (west to east) by thirteen miles (north to south), it has been calculated that the entire population of the world could fit on the IOW, and that it would be like a crowded cocktail party.'

Much of the Island is owned by the National Trust and is completely unspoiled by commercial development. This must be just about the most idyllic setting possible for a Festival of Music. Tourist attractions include Solent yachting, the International Power Boat Race (held on the Festival weekend), and beautiful sandy beaches and coves, 'some of which are frequented by only a handful of people'.

Ironies multiply. It was on some of these very beaches that naked men and women would dance in ritual circles on the sand, while on the golf course above hippie anarchists lived rough, and planned violent revolution. All this, or course, was still to unfold.

By March, things had begun to move towards their inevitable conclusion. As the rock press breathlessly reported – fed facts and rumours by Fiery Creations like seals gulping down raw fish whole – rock acts including Simon And Garfunkle, the Rolling Stones, Richie Havens, and Sly And The Family Stone had received 'feelers'. Plans were rife for Cream to stage a one-off reformation. The Foulks had been in negotiations with the Boulting brothers to make a full-length colour feature film of the entire Festival.

One major name artist would appear on each of the five days. Their spot would now be in the afternoon, to give them two hours to themselves. Rikki Farr further announced that this year's festival would be on a new site, to accommodate an expected 250,000 fans.

> *'The new site will cover three hundred acres and is set up in such a way as to provide people with an entire self-contained community, without infringing on the rights of local inhabitants.'*

The original plan was to hold the Festival at Churchill's Farm, Calbourne, a landlocked site west of Newport, the Island's capital. However, a Select Committee of the County Council found this unsuitable – 'the land is high and is known to be both windy and damp' – but agreed instead to East Afton Farm, Freshwater.

The new site was situated on a flat plain just off the main Newport-Freshwater road in the heart of the quiet and mysterious West Wight. It was overshadowed by the massive chalk bulk of Afton Down and – further to the west – the granite monument to Alfred, Lord Tennyson, and Tennyson Down itself as it curved away to the Needles, and the sea.

Ron 'Turner' Smith:

> *'Ray Foulk and I spent most of the winter, one or two nights a week, talking about it, designing it, drawing it out – until the plan finally evolved. We went across and saw Mark Woodnutt*

about a site, to see if the County Council would join with us. I got the impression that Woodnutt wanted a slice of the action; he thought there was good money to be made.

'Ronnie and Ray joined me over at Woodnutt's house; we had agreed that we were not going to pass any money over to Woodnutt, so he stiffened his opposition. We got a convoy of vehicles to move out to Churchill's Farm where we hoped to pitch our site, when Ray – who had been in County Hall that morning – came steaming down the road to say, "They've blocked us here; we can use a field at Afton Farm." When we saw it, it was obvious they wanted to smash us, because the land was overlooked by Afton Down, and we knew immediately there would be as many people outside as in.'

A far more magical setting, in retrospect, with Tennyson Down outlined behind the stage, and the 'sunset and evening star' spread over the waters where Tennyson wrote 'Crossing The Bar'. It was as if the Victorian poet – whose musical guests included Edward Lear and Jenny Lind, the 'Swedish nightingale', as well as Sir Arthur Sullivan, and whose memory had attracted Dylan the previous year – was beaming down in approval. Perhaps he was!

There are still dark rumours about the reasons behind this change of site. Mark Woodnutt was the sitting Conservative MP for the Island, and would bring in the Isle of Wight Act the next year, ensuring that no such massive happenings would ever disturb the geriatric charms of the Island again.

Woodnutt was later defeated as MP by the Liberal Steve Ross. Some locals still maintain this was partly the result of local feeling against retired warriors like Commander Reese-Millington, who held political power in the Island like a South American junta. Woodnutt was also not helped by his part in the Bembridge Harbour scandal, an unsuccessful plan to develop a beauty spot in the east Wight, not for one-off pop festivals but for housing. Far more acceptable!

As I later found out to my own cost, opposition to any pop event on the Island persists to this day, even among some of the more high-ranking bureaucrats in County Hall. Memories are long on the Isle of Wight. Such opposition is just as prepared to take the law into its own hands as any drug-crazed hippie.

By early June, the only acts definitely booked were the Who, Richie Havens, Chicago, Pentangle and Mungo Jerry. The DJs were to be Rikki Farr and 'blond, bespectacled authority on progressive music', Jeff Dexter. The Beach Boys, Girls Together Outrageously, Terry Reid, Canned Heat, and Eric Burden And War were among the intriguing names considered but never confirmed.

Press Officer Peter Harrigan announced that the Festival was expected to be broadcast to an audience 'approaching World Cup size'. Five European radio stations, plus television units from France, Germany and Switzerland would be covering the event, while American CBS hoped to beam excerpts 'live' to TV and/or cinema screens in the States. The sound system alone would cost £100,000, while there would also be a screening of Bob Dylan's *Festival* film.

Two more star names were soon announced. Jimi Hendrix would fly in from Hawaii, where he was filming *Rainbow Bridge*, for a fee 'in excess of £10,000'. Meanwhile, 'following six months of complicated negotiations', the Doors had also agreed to appear.

In early July, another piece of the jigsaw fell into place when Fiery Creations announced that the top attraction at the Festival would be Joan Baez, 'in the same spot that Dylan occupied on the Sunday night last year', and as an exclusive performance – her first for three years in Britain. As her husband was currently in prison in the States for draft evasion, she had refused to appear in her own country since Woodstock. The Doors would headline on Friday, Hendrix would top the bill on Saturday, and two further names had been added to Sunday's bill – John Sebastian and James Taylor.

Other bookings included Lighthouse – a fifteen piece rock band formed from the Toronto Symphony Orchestra – pop group Arrival, Spirit and Cat Mother, and the All Night News Boys, whose first album had been produced by Hendrix.

Tickets for the weekend would cost £3. Peter Harrigan talked about possible problems, and how they planned to overcome them.

'This is our third festival. For the first one we brought Jefferson Airplane over. We got 10,000 people and the stage was just the back of two lorries. Last year we had Bob Dylan and something like 150,000 came to see him. We were only expecting 50,000 and to be quite honest the facilities – toilets, catering etc – were

strained. We have learned a lot from the past and this year we are planning everything with a figure of 200,000 in mind. If we do get more – and we have carried out surveys; there is a lot of exaggeration with the numbers at pop festivals – there will be relief toilets and things like that ready for use.

'The fact that we are on an Island will help ease the situation; people won't be able to bring their cars over, so we won't have long jams. Ferries will be running all night and local companies are organising the transport to the actual site. There will be large camping areas all around the arena.

'For those who fall ill there will be a full field hospital with over a dozen doctors and forty nurses. There will also be Public Health officers on the site to ensure that the food that is being sold is of a high standard. There is a large warehouse here where all the food for the Festival will be stored. We will be getting plenty of fresh milk every day. In the central kitchens there sill be forty ex Army Catering Corps experts. They know how to deal with big numbers and will be supplying good quality food at a low price.

'We have spent over £100,000 on getting the artists to appear, and about the same on preparing the site. We could have spent less on facilities and made a huge profit, but people would have been disappointed and they wouldn't come again next year. That's not what we want. We want this to become an annual event. We want it to last.'

Meanwhile, Leonard Cohen, Joni Mitchell, the Moody Blues, Family and Taste had all now been confirmed, as had been the debut performance of Emerson, Lake And Palmer. Temporary homes were being arranged for the visiting artists. Leonard Cohen would be living on a yacht and Joan Baez in a country mansion (this later turned out to be hotel in Shanklin).

Six monks from Quarr Abbey had been invited to perform the Gregorian chant for which they are famous, appropriately on Sunday morning. Pete Harrigan also announced that there would be a film of the event, either a documentary or a feature.

'It won't be another Woodstock. This will be something entirely new in cinema.'

The Great South Coast Bankholiday Pop Festivity

to be held at

Hell Field, Ford Farm, Nr. Godshill
ISLE OF WIGHT

August 31st, 1968 6 p.m. to 10 a.m.
All night

The greatest pop festival ever held in this country

The complete festival will be compered by JOHN PEEL
and opened by JIMMY SAVILLE

Guest Artist from the U.S.A.

The Jefferson Airplane
Coming over from America especially for this festival
to make their first live appearance in this country

Topping the bill from Gt. Britain

The Crazy World of Arthur Brown

ALSO

The Move   Plastic Penny   Pretty Things   Tyrannosaurus Rex
The Mirage

Aynsley Dunbar Retaliation   Fairport Convention   Orange Bicycle
Blonde on Blonde   The Smile   The Cherokees   Helcyon Order

Light Show   An incredible multi-screen light show by Students from the R.C.A.

Free Film Shows   Beer Tents   Refreshment Tents

How to get there

Trains leave Waterloo Station at 6 minutes to every hour for Portsmouth Harbour. By road the A3
runs from London to Portsmouth. Ferries from Portsmouth to Ryde take half an hour and run every
half hour. Special Festival buses or coaches will meet all ferries to take passengers to Hell Field

Tickets available from

London Clayman Agency Ltd. Tel. 01 247 5531, 7/8 Aldgate High St., EC3 154 Bishopsgate, EC2
(opposite Liverpool St. Station)   65 Fenchurch St., E.C 3 (opp. Fenchurch St. Station)
Derek's Record's, 8 Aldgate High Street, EC3   Apple Ltd., 94 Baker Street, W1

Isle of Wight Teagues, Newport and Ryde.   Youngs, Cowes, Sandown and Shanklin
John Menzies, Ventnor   Photo-Wight, Freshwater

Bournemouth Minns, 5/7 Gervis Place   Music Box, 23 The Triangle

Southampton Minns, 158 Above Bar   Henry's Record Shop, 116 St. Mary's St.

Brighton Telefusion Ltd., 53 North Street   Hove Travel Agency, Planet House, Church Rd., Hove
50 West Street and 12 Pavilion Buildings   Bredons Bookshop, 3 Bartholomews

Portsmouth & Southsea Portsmouth Radio & Record Centre, 129 Fawcett Road, Fratton
Minns, 67 Osborne Road

Poole Scetchfields Ltd., 21 High Street   **Westbourne** Minns, 68 Poole Road

Winchester Whitwams, 70 High Street   **Chichester** Bagatel Boutique, Crane St.

Worthing Music Shop, 22 New Broadway

Tickets 25s. (or 30s. to include Portsmouth-Ryde return ferry fares)

1968 festival flyer.

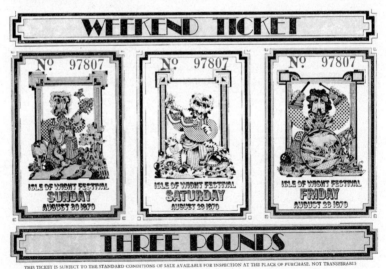

THIS TICKET IS SUBJECT TO THE STANDARD CONDITIONS OF SALE AVAILABLE FOR INSPECTION AT THE PLACE OF PURCHASE. NOT TRANSFERABLE

(Top) 1969 'King Kong' programme.
(Bottom) 1970 festival weekend ticket.

(Top) 1970 Mandala programme.
(Bottom) 1970 reserved enclosure pass.

Notice of public meeting at Freshwater Memorial Hall, 21 July 1970.

(Top) Ray Foulk leaving County Hall with the official document permitting East Afton Farm as the approved venue for the 1970 festival. (Bottom) Jeff Dexter, festival DJ.

(Top) From left to right, Rikki Farr, Ron Foulk, Peter Harrigan and Murray Lerner.
(Bottom) Ron 'Turner' Smith, festival director.

(Top) Afton Farm, before the deluge.
(Bottom) Pop festival HQ, Inglefield, Totland.

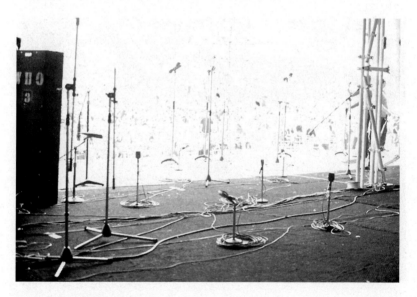

(Top) Festival toilets at Golden Hill Fort being 'run in'.
(Bottom) Afton stage 1970 with vacant mikes.

(Top) Backstage ramp being constructed.
(Bottom) Construction of the security fence, Afton.

(Top) Entrance to Afton site.
(Bottom) Relaxing, Afton site.

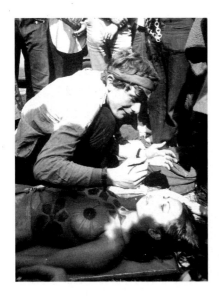

(Top) Relaxing, Compton Bay.
(Bottom) Body painting, Afton.

(Top) Feeding the 500,000.
(Bottom) Fresh fruit stand, Afton.

(Top) Donovan and young friends on stage.
(Bottom) St John's Ambulance Brigade at the ready.

(Top) Daily Express balloon, used for aerial shots in Murray Lerner's film.
(Bottom) The packed arena with Afton Down behind.

Security guards.

Cleaning up.

Well, he was right, but in a way that he could never have predicted, a funeral lament for the sixties.

On 31 July, local television showed the first view of the East Afton site, with one of George Weeks' lorries turning in. The first set of battle lines were already being drawn. As local opposition began to stir – mainly over the provision of toilet facilities, and the danger of a hippie invasion into the rural beauties of the West Wight – the vicar of Mottistone set up a multi-faith team of ministers to provide religious services and councilling.

The Revd Bowyer's role as mediator was soon to be needed far more urgently at an event which, for some locals, still overshadows the pop festival itself; the extraordinary scenes of civil war at Freshwater Memorial Hall. A solid brick building, its foundation stone was laid by Hallam, Lord Tennyson, and the fund-raising for its construction initiated by Julia Margaret Cameron, whose photographs line its walls.

Here was enacted the timeless conflict between rebellious youth and the ruling village elders. Commander Reece-Millington's fears of 'black power' – or was that black magic – and communism lurking in the background seemed about to become fact.

As the local newspaper headlined the story on 18 July:

'On Friday night, a meeting of Freshwater people was broken up in disorder.'

A crowd of more than 650 people had filled the Memorial Hall and overflowed into the car park and the street. Loudspeakers were erected outside. There were angry scenes at the door when local people were refused admission to the hall because it was full. They pointed out that many inside came from places other than the West Wight. In the hall itself, the left side was taken mainly by pro-festival, younger people in their colourful clothes and long hair, and the right side by older residents, like guests at an ill-matched wedding.

When Brigadier Phipps, County Council representative for Freshwater, took the stage there was uproar. Among those with him were the wonderfully named Admiral Sir Manley Power – who sported a monocle – and Mr Cawdell of the Vectis Nationalist Party, a kind of Island Klu Klux Klan, without the hoods. As he tried to explain why the meeting had been called, Brigadier Phipps was drowned out by shouts, catcalls and a constant stream of interruptions and expletives.

Brigadier Phipps went on to say that Afton was a fine site, and Mr Clarke the owner was with them that evening. Mr Clarke had made it quite clear that he did not intend to have the Festival on his land unless all officials were satisfied. Fiery Creations Ltd had said they were prepared to provide all the required facilities. 'We hope this has been said in good faith,' he said.

The meeting again burst into uproar when he tried to introduce Rear-Admiral Clarke to talk on the Bath Festival at Shepton Mallet. Rikki Farr, who had been continually objecting, got up on the stage. He stood in front of the brigadier, who was still trying to talk, and eventually was offered the microphone. It was taken back from him after a few minutes, when Brigadier Phipps accused him of talking propaganda.

Conditions were now so bad that the brigadier announced, like Graham Chapman in *Monty Python* when things were getting too silly, 'This meeting is out of hand and I greatly regret it is closed.' The brigadier and his party now swept out of the hall, in high dudgeon. Rikki Farr took over the microphone and was joined on the stage by some of the promoters, as well as Mr Clarke. Farr made the first of many emotional public pronouncements over the next two months.

> *'I have no real right to stand here... I feel a complete pirate. If I can, I appoint myself chairman. There has been a huge investment in this Festival, in which there will not be as much pop as last year. We have, in a way, worked against ourselves by the action taken tonight.'*

A beacon of sense, the Revd Bowyer now came forward to take the chair. By this time half of the people had left, including most of the Festival's opponents. Rival petitions were produced, and Mr Cawdwell said there was widespread fear of trespass, violation of property and lack of proper hygiene. If the numbers were limited to 50,000, some of his fears would be allayed.

Both sides regrouped their forces, but the battle lines were now firmly drawn. However, on 23 July the formal agreement – between the IOW County Council and Fiery Creations – that the Festival could take place was duly signed. Ron Smith:

'It took three or four weeks to build the basic site; we set up a workshop in an old button factory in Middleton, where we constructed fibre-glass loo seats. We had nine diggers on the site, and piped several miles of ditches, as well as a hundred taps and stand-pipes, and over a thousand loos, built over deep trenches. At that time, the water supply for all of Freshwater was restricted to one eight-inch main at the foot of the Down so they tapped some supplies that had been used in the Crimean War on top of Headon Warren and added this to the system, as well as some brackish water which came from Freshwater pumping station.

'Much to my regret now, we also removed a couple of miles of fences – we fetched in scaffolding from all over the country – and of course we had French, Italian and Spanish anarchists camping there. One night, they decided to break the fence down. I was called to the scene, met their leaders and talked them into a quiet mood, and sent Ronnie for some Mars Bars, which I distributed free – and it shut 'em up.

'The Festival went on. The editor of a leading architects' magazine was overwhelmed by it all. "You're building a small city here!" He devoted that month's main article to the pop festival.

'The scene, I thought, was fantastic; there were lots of people in Freshwater who had been dead against it who made a packet! The local pubs and supermarket just couldn't get enough supplies in – deliveries were coming in all day long and going out as soon as they came.

'It was estimated by Sealink that well over 300,000 people had come over; they didn't even bother to count the number going back, just pushed them all onto the boats like sardines, standing up on the open decks of the car ferries, and shipped them off like that just to get them off the Island.

'We had people coming over from Woodstock to work on that stage; they said our Festival was far larger and better organised than Woodstock, which was – for anyone in the know – a complete washout. Ours was a triumph of organisation and good music.'

Further details were revealed of this new venue:

'The site comprises several hundred acres of natural grassland, and commands extensive views of the English Channel, the mainland coast, and Tennyson Down.'

The thirty-eight acre grass arena was to be completely surrounded by nine inch high double walling, between which a ring road would run, allowing shops and other amenity areas to be serviced. There would be complete catering facilities and every type of food and refreshment would be available from over eighty serving areas, including restaurants. Licensed bars would open, on site, from 11 am to 11 pm.

Elaborate sanitation arrangements were to include over 1,200 closets, half a mile of urinals and a hundred water points. Litter would be dealt with by using over 2,500 waste-paper sacks daily and a continuous sanitation and disposal service.

There was to be a special welfare enclosure, a fully equipped field hospital, a church tent, a Release tent – for those suffering bad trips – and a police-controlled lost property office.

Ferries would operate a twenty-four hour shuttle service to Ryde (from 21 August) and would there connect with buses running directly to the site. Extra night trains would run from Waterloo if necessary.

Over 300 acres were to be available for camping space, free of charge for people, and marquees for people with no tent of their own. On sale at the site were to be disposable sleeping bags, made of paper and foam rubber. With unconscious humour, it was stated that these had been tested under arctic conditions and should last in the Island climate for at least a week.

Meanwhile, the musical details of the Festival were swimming into shape. On 1 August, Ten Years After and Jethro Tull were added to the line up: Tull had not played in Britain for almost a year, and neither band would be playing any other British gigs for the conceivable future. The pot of gold for English progressive bands, the kind who had spent their early years playing the back rooms of pubs for a pittance, was to be found playing large concert halls and colleges in the States.

Ron Foulk announced that, 'People are depending on this Festival to revive their faith in these events. There have been so many bad festivals recently.' He also announced the move to Afton. 'It's a very nice site, with the sea on one side and a forest on the other.'

One disappointment was that James Taylor had cancelled his appearance to work on a film *Two-Lane Blacktop*, also ironically a lament for sixties freedom, which declines into habit. At the end of the film, the celluloid seems to burn up the in projector. Ticket sales remained buoyant and flooded in to Festival HQ, PO Box 1, Freshwater.

On 8 August, it was announced that Miles Davis had definitely signed for a one-and-a-half hour appearance on the Saturday bill. A musical pathfinder since the days of bebop, Miles had recently played at big rock venues like the Hollywood Bowl and Fillmore East. His current double album, *Bitches Brew*, added electronic amplification without impairing the melancholy and majesty of his own solos; indeed it gave a new context to the greatest jazzman of his age.

An official theme song for the event, 'Let The World Wash In', by a new group called I Luv Wight was released on 14 August, although it would be jettisoned at the Festival itself for a rock guitar instrumental based on a hymn, 'Amazing Grace', by the Great Awakening.

In another universe, the clerk to Freshwater Parish Council was carefully monitoring public reaction. I have removed full names to protect the guilty.

2 AUGUST

Revd B. called at Mrs A's house (chairman of Parish Council)... said he had had a message to see her; this was not accurate and she informed him so. Following this, her phone rang many times and each time she heard only heavy breathing.

10 AUGUST

Mrs J. reported that hippies, near the monument on Afton Down, urinated in full view of her family without any sense of decency: she also reported fouling and smell under the wall at Military Road.

12 AUGUST

Mr J. reported re Compton Bus Shelter: hippies had slept there... When the RDC man made his routine call to clean it out, the hippies were obstructive, insolent and also caused damage to his vehicle.

13 AUGUST

Re Footpath 28, Desolation Row. Many visits made to this public footpath; obstructions by tents and made-up shelters hard to describe: again, much fouling, trees hacked down, all kinds of rubbish from nearby dump being used as cooking utensils and so on. Two weeks earlier Mrs A. and others had walked this path – and also Footpath 31 – and considered them to be of lovely appearance and a joy to walk. Complete disaster that they are now so destroyed; expressions of 'what will they be like when the pop festival is over'.

14 AUGUST

Mr H. reported that hippies had undressed in launderette and the general customers had been much upset by such behaviour – though they did not make proper complaint. Mr M. said that there were many reports of pilfering in local shops.

15 AUGUST

Mrs P. of Guyers Road informed me that on Sunday evening at 9.20 pm, hippies had called begging for food – rice, potatoes, bread. Lionel O. said he had been approached by promoters for 'horsemen to act as security guards along the bridle road'.

16 AUGUST

Rotary Well at Freshwater Bay. On Sunday hippies seen by Revd D. removing money from the well.

17 AUGUST

Hippies seen shattering fruit from overhanging trees on to highway at Gate Lane... considered a traffic hazard.

18 AUGUST

Hippies long-legged and lounging across pavements in many parts of the village: many old and infirm people were forced to manoeuvre through feet and legs to get past, very often having to step onto the highway. This was especially noticeable in the areas of the Royal Standard Hotel, post office, supermarket, newsagent, public conveniences and so on. People on holiday felt (and stated emphatically) that the pop festival fans received special favour, it being hopeless to try to get stamps at the post office, use a telephone, or go to a public convenience... and it certainly wasn't possible to sit down on a public seat. There were many reports of long queues at Moa Place convenience, and of 'impatient' hippies using the school green grassland for the purpose: several reports of the pop fans saying the pop site lavatories were in a bad condition.

18 AUGUST
Hippies slept in every available bus shelter, public convenience (with men in Ladies!), council vehicles, hotel porches and so on – waste paper baskets used as pillows; refused to move on when requested. The general public were waiting for buses in extremely bad weather and could not shelter, as usual, under cover. Several people reported seeing a baby being washed in ditches and streams; also that a very battered old car at the dump was being used as a tent by young hippies with a small baby. Hippies sleeping at Freshwater Bay Esplanade shelter – removed by RDC men. Each hippie then urinated on beach or sea wall in full view of everyone there. RSPCA box stolen from post office.

20 AUGUST
Extensive walk over Afton Down. No obstruction now of Footpath 31 or 28, though on latter much more 'camping' in the hedges, many with fires; a lot more trees hacked away. Evidence of camping on side of the Down with more tree hacking, clearly heard. Saw plenty of hippies helping themselves to hay stacks; also saw farmer and bailiff trying to retrieve some of these (and heard later they were being sold at two shillings each). The barbed wire fence, National Trust/Golf Course land, severed in many places already.

Mrs P. Hippies knocked at her door at 11 pm asking for candles. She lives alone, pretended speaking to husband and said she had none.

Shacks installed at Station Road (Indian beads, coke etc) also hot dog vans hanging around for sites. More shacks, vans etc along middle Newport road, and in fields near the Thorley Road corner.

Made a personal tour of the Freshwater district. Many faces held a look of concern and anxiety, some even hatred, for what councillors and clerk had 'allowed to happen to normal peaceful condition'.

Back in the wider world, Fiery Creations continued to bombast the news media. They had now arranged for two additional concerts for the 26th and 27th of August. Ticket sales had topped the 50,000 mark and already hundreds of fans were arriving on the camping site, many of them from overseas. Around 20,000 tickets had been sold overseas – mainly in Europe and the USA, where package trips to the Festival were being organised. A minority hard-core opposition to the event continued locally; one suspected cadres of the Vectis Nationalist Army. A weekend's organised sabotage to the site caused £500 worth of damage, and several threatening letters were received by Fiery Creations staff. One letter, postmarked Shanklin, IOW, simply read, 'The first group on stage will be shot'.

Said compere and show producer Rikki Farr, son of boxer Tommy Farr, and due to be the first man on stage:

> *'The event and the thousands who attend it will show this bigoted and hysterical minority that young people can behave responsibly. We are sure the majority of the Island will welcome the fans.'*

He should perhaps have been looking more closely at the 'enemy within'.

Meanwhile, discussions with the Boultings having presumably terminated, Murray Lerner, the American film maker had flown in to direct a full length colour feature film of the Afton Festival. This would...

> *'...cover the preparations for the Event, the hardcore and hysterical opposition against which the organisers, Fiery Creations, are battling as well as full coverage of the whole Festival period. Cameras will follow artists and fans from the Continent and America.'*

No one could have known at the time that it would be twenty-five years before highlights of this filming gained a public release, or that by then it would be a time capsule into a vanished world, in the process of being undermined by guerrilla action and principled violence. The real battle had hardly commenced.

Lerner had originally been booked to attend the British premiere of *Festival*, his documentary of the Newport folk festivals, which had won the San Giorga Award at the Venice Film Festival of 1967. It included the footage of the legendary occasion when Dylan first went electric, and also featured Joan Baez and Donovan – both appearing at the IOW – Johnny Cash, Peter, Paul And Mary, Howlin' Wolf, Judy Collins, Pete Seeger and Buffy Saint Marie.

One great disappointment was that the Grateful Dead would not now be appearing on the Isle of Wight bill, as earlier hoped. They were due to arrive in England as part of a caravan moving across from San Francisco to New York to the Isle of Wight. Last minute 'hassles' forced them to cancel. With the death in August 1995 of Jerry Garcia, such a trip can never now be completed.

Another dream died during the weeks leading up to the Festival, that of establishing the Island as a perennial festival attraction. Again using the World War II terminology beloved of Fiery Creations, Peter Harrigan announced that...

> '...September 1 is "D Day" for next weekend's IOW Festival; "Decision" day, when organisers will learn whether a full-time site can be set up for future years. Or if they will be forced to scrap the annual event altogether. It's really up to the fans now. If everyone pulls their weight and behaves, then we'll be laughing. We have to show the opposition that we're capable of staging a festival properly. Otherwise, in view of local problems and the mood against the festivals sweeping the country at the moment, this will be the LAST Isle of Wight.'

A more parochial problem also had arisen. The Moody Blues had dropped out due to a dispute about billing. A spokesman for the pop promoters attempted conciliation: 'We'd welcome them back. The billing business has unfortunately been blown up a bit.' The order of billing, and size of the band's name on publicity material, had deteriorated into a bare-knuckle scrap between various agents and managers to establish a pecking order, a divine order from superstars like Dylan and Hendrix down to the Judas Jumps of this world. It was really like adolescent boys comparing their dimension.

Moodies' flautist Ray Thomas however made the whole dispute a matter of principle. 'In our opinion, the IOW is not being conducted in the best interests of music or the fans.' And to compensate their fans, the Moodies planned a special free show in London. The Everly Brothers were rapidly confirmed as a replacement. The Moodies soon came back into the fold, and ate their words, which is just as well as 'Nights In White Satin' – performed at twilight – was one of the highlights of the whole Festival.

It is almost a relief to return to the simple world of the Freshwater parish clerk. Here is the sort of man who could report the sinking of the *Titanic* as displacing a lot of water, and causing needless damage to a perfectly formed iceberg, while worrying about possible improprieties in the mixed lifeboats.

25 AUGUST

Every seat and piece of grass 'taken over' by hippies – litter everywhere in the village, a couldn't-care-less attitude by all fans, baskets and bins being completely ignored. Bread in short supply. Buses filled by hippies with no chance for public. Considerable human excrement over side of Downs (Mrs A., who reported this, felt and looked quite ill). I had to phone Health Department and ask for it to be disinfected because of the stench. Mrs T. of The Artist reported eighteen brooches missing after two or three hippies had been in her shop. Now a considerable crop of all sorts of inferior trading vans in many parts, leaving considerable litter nearby. Mr F., High Street, reported an indecency outside his shop at 8 am. He told those involved the village was not used to such behaviour and he would send for police if they did not move on.

26 AUGUST

Noise – all night Discotecque (sic).

27 AUGUST

Took a walk over Afton Down; very few pop fans in the actual arena, but plenty on the hillside. Footpath 28 (Desolation Row) a dreadful looking sight.

28 AUGUST

Mr C. reported that in mid-afternoon he saw sexual indecency at a culvert, near side of Afton Manor gate.

29 AUGUST

Mrs H. reported that at 10.30 pm a stark naked man jumped out and danced in front of her car.

30 AUGUST

Reports of extensive nude bathing at Compton Beach: did Police ignore this sort of thing? Mrs A. witnessed one nude couple who passed her by to be saying, 'There's nothing else left for kicks.'

The Arena looked squalid, with large piles of rubbish, tins and so on at various points among the fans; the lower site was oozing and squelching near the water taps and it was a relief to step onto the highway. We had left our son there, and he later went into the Arena for several hours... it was interesting that he too wanted everything washed after he returned home.

Parish clerk

The media was also quick to concentrate on the tons of rubbish left, which while in itself unpleasant – though scarcely as dangerous as industrial waste or nuclear fall out – was quickly cleared up, mainly by hippies to pay for their ferry fares back home.

What these accounts omit is the atmosphere of friendliness which prevailed throughout, both on and off site. Most locals who I have since spoken to identified some of these complainants as notorious old busybodies. Many remember the Festival as a piece of living history which brought much needed trade to the village, and a touch of excitement to the West Wight.

Such encounters could also be genuinely disturbing.

'1 Gentleman, in state of apparent agitation, black eye, bruised swollen knuckles, knocked on door.
'2 He said, "I'm Doctor Robin Farquarson. May I use your phone to contact my family. I'll reverse the charge."
'3 Permission was granted, as I supposed, erroneously, that there had been an accident.
'4 He phoned a Fleet Street number which proved to be The Sun.
'5 He asked them to give a message to "his mate", Deyv Shaap. He repeated the message in rhyme, "in code", he said. The Sun *would not accept it without investigation, so he rang off.*

'6 He then rang another number and revealed that he was a White Panther and that the Panthers and Hells Angels had pulled down the fence etc. The last lines of the coded message were, "See you in White, Saturday night, mission accomplished."

'7 When challenged about the cost of the calls he offered to write on a piece of paper that he owed us five shillings, or he would give us a ballpoint pen. He departed, leaving an empty boot box, and declaring "Peace and love".

'8 I phoned the police, but nothing transpired.'

I can add to this that Dr Robin Farquarson was a friend of Rupert Murdoch, future owner of *The Sun*, and a brilliant research scientist. He subsequently became a 'drop out', the title of his autobiography. He died in the early seventies, a hard-line hippie activist, who barely survived the decade which matched his politics and his madness.

The parish archives contain other forms of selfishness masquerading as social concern. Here is part of the grandly titled *Reflections Of A Resident Of Afton Road.*

'Why did the fans have to use Afton Road en route to Freshwater at the rate of 1,500 an hour? Why were the shops so crowded, even early in the morning, that it was difficult and unpleasant to shop? My small granddaughter, aged three, who could not be said to be prejudiced (unlike her grandfather) *had sleepless and disturbed nights, for even when the music and words could not be distinguished the drum beats were disturbing.'*

That must remain a matter of opinion. For many young people who attended – myself included – the long weekend provided exactly that, an image of a better world which reality has never quite matched. The experience of Afton has been etched forever on the minds and hearts of all those lucky enough to have been there. It happened like this...

Festival Log

September 1969 to August 1970

30 September, 1969
Toronto Peace Festival
Ontario, Canada
John Lennon and a Plastic Ono Band which contains Eric Clapton on lead guitar and Yoko – screaming – appear alongside rock 'n' roll legends Little Richard, Chuck Berry, Bo Diddley and Gene Vincent.

6 December, 1969
Altamont, California
As the film *Let It Bleed* testifies, the English Hells Angels are a pale shadow of their American counterparts. A hastily arranged free festival, this degenerates into an orgy of violence and death; among the mayhem Jefferson Airplane and the Flying Burrito Brothers put in an appearance. The Rolling Stones' set was cut short. Symbolically, the end of sixties innocence.

23 May, 1970
Plumpton Pop Festival
A two-day event featuring Tom Rush, May Blitz, Audience, Warm Dust, and Van Der Graaf Generator.

26–27 June, 1970
The Bath Festival Of Blues And Progressive Music
Shepton Mallet
Led Zeppelin, Fairport, Johhny Winter, Flock, the Mothers Of Invention, Santana, and the Byrds – who had to play an acoustic set in driving rain. There was an impromptu free festival held outside, with Pink Floyd playing on the back of a lorry.

3–5 July, 1970
Atlanta Pop Festival
Georgia
Captain Beefheart, Jimi Hendrix, Ginger Baker's Airforce and local hopefuls the Allmann Brothers Band.

August 1970
Pilton Festival
Small-scale event held by local dairy farmer Michael Eaves. T. Rex headlined. Precursor of the Glastonbury Festival, which started properly the next year, and ushered in a new generation of outdoor festivals, with an ecological basis.

August 1970
Krumlin, Yorkshire
Around 25,000 fans endure atrocious weather. Sitting on an exposed moor, they suffer howling gales and freezing rain. A combination of bad organisation and promoters' greed.

26–30 August, 1970
Third Isle Of Wight Festival
Afton Farm, Freshwater
Quite the opposite. The 'Last Event'.

8

'Oh brave new world'

I drive past the 1970 Festival site most days. It's under cultivation now, a vast plain rich in wheat and barley. The only human constituents of the scene are the occasional farm worker hidden in his tractor or a lone windsurfer hanging seemingly motionless over Afton Down. And yet half a million people once made this place home, stretched as far as the eye could see in a kaleidoscope of colour and excitement. British Rail subsequently announced that over 600,000 people had used their ferries during the Festival period.

They came by foot, on motor cycles, in cars and vans, some painted with bright designs and provocative slogans, 'Woodstock nation' on the move. By Friday, every ferry rode low in the water under the weight of the seemingly never-ending hordes of fans, all coming to see an international line-up of artists unequalled in this country before or since. I queued with my boy-scout tent and father's ARP blanket at Lymington Quay, then took a bus from Yarmouth to the Festival site.

Although I had bought my ticket in advance, the sound was best from up on Afton Down, a natural amphitheatre seating upwards of 50,000 people, and soon nicknamed Desolation Hill. Below were tents of every conceivable shape and colour, many surmounted with a flag to establish their owner's identity. I remember coming back to mine in the dark to find it had fallen over in the wind. Some made their own form of dwelling, with sheets of polythene and wood, others with bales of hay. Loud music played until dawn. Each morning, like a Hollywood epic projected onto the downs, an even larger multitude thronged the green fields as far as the eye could see. *'Oh brave new world/that has such people in it.'* It seemed it might last forever...

9

Wednesday 27 August, 1970

Things were a bit chaotic around the press tent where no lights had come on and the cool custodian, a Mr Everest, had gone to fix a generator. There were already a few thousand people in the arena, and the proceedings went on merrily until midnight, records interspersing the live acts. As one early bird recalls:

'Radio Geronimo played records of guest groups throughout. During the first two days, some of the booked groups didn't play – very chaotic and lots of sound problems. It was like a big boy-scout camp, with people lending things. I camped by the woods to get firewood...'

Canvas City – an enormous marquee, 180 feet long by 60 feet wide – hosted Pete Brown of the Electric Cinema, DJs Simon Stable and Vince Dunn with his Black Sun Light Circus, plus James Hamilton, alias 'Dr Soul', all for a small admission charge. DJ Penny Valentine recalls...

'...a quaint, almost village-like atmosphere. Areas of green grass, yet to be covered with sleeping bags and empty coke tins, were still visible.'

Having two free warm-up days was a wise move. Firstly it gave the ever-growing crowd something pleasant to listen to in the later summer sunshine, and secondly it enabled the superhuman posse of technicians to sort out the giant banks of speakers. With the organisers taking complete control over lesser-known acts, the music came thick and fast, yet always ended on time.

Many acts were forced to stop while running repairs were made on the equipment, but the growing crowd was promised good and efficient days ahead. One jaundiced commentator noted that many of these groups had been slung onto the bill less for their ability but through deals between the promoters and various backscratchers, 'The managers with more than one "interest", the record companies with an "interest", the big-time reporter with an "interest".' Of whom...

JUDAS JUMP

An early, and junior league, supergroup drawn from members of the Alan Bown Set and Amen Corner. The low spot of their set was an awful version of – perhaps appropriately – 'Jumping Jack Flash'. They certainly soon took the long jump into oblivion.

ROSALIE SORRELS

A young American folk singer, managed by a friend of Bob Dylan. One of the highlights of the day was her backing guitarist, Dave Bromberg, who played some incredibly slow, almost talking blues, and was invited back to do a solo spot.

> *'Rosalie Sorrells is a dark-eyed mountain girl from Boise, Idaho, with a face like an elf and a voice that reminds some people of Billie Holiday.'*
> Programme note

Bromberg's version of 'Mr Bojangles' appears on the *First Great Rock Festivals Of The Seventies* triple LP.

KATHY SMITH

An American girl singer, just her voice and guitar, who went down well.

KRIS KRISTOFFERSON

His material all jogged along at the same mid-tempo, while 'Blame It On The Stones', which offered a mild rebuke to Mick Jagger, did nothing to increase his popularity with the crowd. Then light-years away from being a superstar actor, he played his guitar to as many people knocking the scaffolding together as he did to punters. He returned later in the weekend to a less than ecstatic reception.

> *'Kristofferson is a story-teller and a poet. His lyrics are simple, but filled with intricate details and simple country truths. He talks in long, seemingly rambling, but very together sentences. His song lyrics sometimes come out the same way, passing quickly, leaving their message.'*
> Programme note

The first issue of the Freek Press's free newsletter, dateline Friday, pointed out that 'the first display of empathy amongst the people gathered together had to be a display in noisy dislike of Kris Kristofferson'. It was now that Rikki Farr made his infamous diatribe – 'Now listen here and listen good...' – in protest at the American's reception, and not at the end of the Festival, as the chronology of *Message To Love* suggests. The film shows Kristofferson storming off stage either now or on his second appearance, while his band play on. 'Blame It On The Stones' and 'The Pilgrim – Chapter 33' appear on the *First Great Rock Festivals Of The Seventies* triple LP.

MIGHTY BABY

Ex mod group the Action, Mighty Baby 'belted out the right sounds' through a battery of amps, and lit up the darkness, playing mainly songs, but ending with their half-hour version of John Coltrane's 'India', looser and more improvised, with which the audience joined in on percussion!

By 1970, Mighty Baby's free-wheeling essentially uncommercial music was already becoming an anachronism. Techno-flash and pointless instrumental virtuosity were now all the rage: 'progressive rock' had become big business, with all that entailed. Twenty five years on, though, their legend shines bright. A live version of 'India' appears as 'A Blanket In My Muesli' on the *Glastonbury Fayre* triple LP: it was

115

also to form the centrepiece of their second LP, *The Day Of The Soup* – announced in the Bath Festival programme, but never released. One of the great lost LPs of all time.

Guitarist Martin Stone had appeared a few years before on the Island, in a blues club backing John Lee Hooker. With Chilli Willi, he was a central figure in the early days of pub rock, and played sessions for Stiff records. Now living and recording in Paris, he remains one of the few men alive who can make the lead guitar laugh! Alan 'Bam' King went on to join Ace; his chugging rhythm guitar fuels their single 'How Long'. The other three, all now members of the Sufi faith, were last seen backing Richard Thompson in his Islamic 1977 tour, the most disturbing, spiritual music heard on a British stage since, well, John Coltrane.

Backstage, the grassed enclosure saw much professional posing and sartorial beggar my neighbour. The start of the early seventies obsession with fashion which Roxy Music and Bowie turned into an art form, but which sat ill at odds with the would-be egalitarianism of the times. This *bonhomie* did not always extend to the artists, to whom the prolonged waiting to appear on stage, as the running order got later and later, became an exquisite torture. The folk singer Melanie later told Penny Valentine that she had found the event petrifying, and saw no one there that she knew. She remembered just one person who had befriended her and treated her to some hospitality in his caravan. She only found out afterwards that he was Keith Moon.

10

Thursday 28 August, 1970

On stage, Rikki Farr was saying sensible things to the crowd; 'Such a pleasant looking blond with a very good speaking voice to go with his looks', as the *New Musical Express* commented. The day's line up included two survivors from the 1969 event, the ever present GARY FARR and EVERYONE, basically Liverpool Scene without Adrian Henri, both of whom gave a good account of themselves.

SUPERTRAMP

A new and unknown band, Supertramp, played a long set around teatime. Despite confessing on stage that their act was far from perfect, they particularly impressed with their version of 'All Along The Watchtower'. Unlike Hendrix three days later, they managed to remember the words! *Melody Maker* considered:

> *'There is a pleasing cleanness and precision about their work, and the vocals show sensitivity, but at this juncture they appear to have little that is novel to offer.'*

Shows how wrong critics can be.

This was the original line up, with Richard Palmer on lead guitar. Supertramp went on to become superstars, but for me they never recaptured the melancholy and intellect of their first album.

GILBERTO GIL AND CAENTANO VELOSO

Brazilian musicians Gilberto Gil and Caentano Veloso had been on a European tour with Sergio Mendes. This was the first example of the audience invading the stage, though in this case at the insistence of the organisers, who had seen them dancing in the press enclosure all inside one big jumper, and immediately gave them a spare slot in the afternoon.

With thirteen friends, eleven of whom clapped and sang while half-hidden in a gargantuan party-sized red plastic dress, they beat out half an hour's beautiful bossa nova. Then, one by one, those in the red dress emerged, naked but coyly avoiding full fronted exposure, as they swayed off stage in time to the music, leaving behind a delighted audience.

Gil and Veloso had developed 'tropicalismo', a musical movement in Brazil in the late sixties which led to direct confrontation with the military regime, a regime rather more oppressive than, say, Fiery Creations.

Notable for its use of rock rhythms and dense, oblique lyrics, this new music was at first attacked by audiences and the press as being unpatriotic, rather like punk rock here. Both stars were exiled to England in 1971, but Gil has since become a leading Salvador singer and an increasingly important politician, while Caentano is a kind of Leonardo da Vinci of Brazilian popular culture.

All without the help of the White Panthers!

BLACK WIDOW

Satanic rockers. They were uninspiring until their third-from-last number, which was basically an instrumental piece lasting fifteen minutes with good interaction between guitar and organ, the two players raising and lowering the temperature with considerable skill. Their best known song, 'Come To The Sabbat' – played in brilliant sunshine – provoked the greatest audience response, and earned them an encore. The crowd enjoyed their 'weirdo music', although they performed minus black magic rituals, banned by the organisers. The drummer went on to play with arch-Satanists Showaddywaddy!

GROUNDHOGS

One of the highlights of the first two days. Featured some excellent bass guitar work from Pete Cruikshank and the splendid 'Eccentric Man' from their *Thank Christ For The Bomb* LP. Mainman Tony McPhee later re-formed the band, but recently suffered a minor heart attack.

TERRY REID

The best act in sight on Thursday, and one of the most accomplished of the entire Festival. Reid displayed an impressive range, cutting through from really heavy numbers to quiet, subtle pieces, and even the occasional bossa nova. His voice had a keening, wistful quality, which exactly complemented the slide guitar of Rick Charles, and which he used to good effect on Dylan's 'To Be Alone With You'. His band featured David Lindley – of the American psychedelic band Kaleidoscope, and later right-hand musician to Jackson Browne – and ex Steve Miller drummer Tim Davis. He was last to play, and the show closed down for the day in the 'small hours'.

Terry Reid has never fulfilled his potential as one of Britain's greatest rock singers, in the same super-league as Joe Cocker or Rod Stewart. Albums like *Seed Of Memory* show off his emotional, all defences down style at his best, which combined with his sensitive lyrics should be enough for world fame, but isn't. One of the many gigs he turned down was that of lead singer in a new band emerging from the ashes of the Yardbirds – Led Zeppelin. The same band were also turned down for the Godshill event because of their outrageous fee – £125.

Meanwhile, the real action was off stage. Mike Plumbley recalls watching Supertramp from Afton Down.

> *'There were labourers up there trying to erect fences to block the growing number of punters who were taking advantage of the perfect sound reception and comfort of the hill. It certainly beat being squashed in the compound, and it was free.'*

The *Portsmouth Evening News* for Friday reported a 'battle at IW iron curtain' when fighting broke out between an estimated 800 fans, most of them French, confronting a wall of security guards full on. 'They hurled pieces of piping, scaffolding, bricks and stones at the guards', who in retaliation set their dogs loose, and four fans were badly bitten.

Workmen had begun constructing a nine foot corrugated iron fence in fear of an injunction from the National Trust.

There was a real danger that the Festival would be called off, especially after anarchists had also tried to break up one of the pay boxes containing six girls selling tickets for the weekend. It is this violence – taking place before the Festival had really begun – which forms the climax of Murray Lerner's film. Perhaps it was symbolically, but in reality man of the people, that Ron Smith – with interpreter – approached the free French and rapidly discerned that they were almost starving. A van load of free Kit-Kats staved off trouble for the time being, although these protests rumbled on until the gates were opened on Sunday afternoon.

This was fuelled by free bulletins put out by the White Panthers (*aka* Mick Farren and two friends) and the Freek Press conglomerate: *Oz*, *Friends*, *Ink* and *International Times*. Typical headlines included 'VD Scare Is Bullshit', 'Backstage Groupie News' and 'Con Men Caterers'. Useful, but hardly a Fiery Creations fanzine. Never underestimate the power of a good grudge. Farren had made firm enemies with Rikki Farr after the latter had booked him at his Birdcage club in Portsmouth with his band the Social Deviants. A band, it must be said, who always lacked a good tune.

After the French Secret Service sunk a Greenpeace boat – and the murderers who perpetuated it were later given official honours – one harbours all kinds of suspicions about the true identity of some of these 'anarchists'. Certainly the French government were violently opposed to pop festivals in their own country.

On the other hand, such disruptive tactics were part of the creed of 'deconstruction' then emerging from post-revolutionary Paris. No longer was any member of an audience a passive consumer, the emphasis was now on his or her response, and not the elite preoccupations of the artist.

Under the generic term 'reception theory', this idea has had a profound impact on the study of all forms of art, turning the focus away from the performer to the performed to. Perhaps the first acting out of this new intellectual egalitarianism (usually couched by its practitioners in impenetrable jargon) was at the Isle of Wight. Or perhaps people just wanted a good old-fashioned punch up.

11

Friday 29 August, 1970

By Friday, things really began to take shape. A seat at the front became a prize possession, and campers prepared themselves for the delights to come. The press enclosure was dense with bodies hanging from the stage, cameras thrusting forward, while the fenced perimeter gyrated and flexed, dripping with eager enthusiasts. The mayhem intensified with nightfall. *Record Mirror* painted the scene in prose of violent day-glo:

> *'Beaming light towers like prison camp spires lent electric lustre to freaking patrons who appeared and disappeared suddenly from the forests of hair. They floated and hopped like midnight maidens set upon by midnight madness, roving in and out of the fluorescent cigarette smoke that hung over the fields like a 1932 vampire movie. In the murky distance was "Devastation Hill", where hippies of iron reclined at forty-five degree slants, some upside down, allowing gravity to help the blood to their heads faster. Just over the hill was the rich green sea where afternoons saw young sirens bouncing in the waves, their chests bulging forth free in the summer surf. Most of the*

rest of them bulged forth free too. "Excellent vibrations,"
chuckled a frustrated old farmer to himself. "George! Get away
from that beach," bellowed his threatening wife.'

Back on dry land, a Napoleonic feat of organisation saw a whole new
city arise on the bare fields of Afton. Milton Keynes had nothing on
this! Despite at least one attempt already at mass sabotage, a work-
force of 400 had by now completed work on the site, a thirty-eight
acre grass arena surrounded by nine foot high double walls. A ring
road ran between them, allowing safe access for goods – and
equally safe removal of cash – for the hundred shops and eighty
'refreshment areas'. The stage itself was the largest ever built
outdoors in Britain. There were 1,200 WCs, half a mile of urinals and
a hundred water points, tapping into the reservoir buried in the
chalk of Afton Down.

Around 300 acres had been laid aside for camping, and amenities
included a church tent and a police-controlled lost property office. The
greatest wonder was a twenty-four hour shuttle service from
Portsmouth to Ryde. *Those* were the days.

Murray Lerner had arrived with a large film crew. CBS had set up
twenty-four track recording facilities for its own acts, and ended up
taping the whole event. The results of both endeavours would largely
lie unseen and unheard for the next twenty-five years, buried gold.

A special Festival programme featuring Dave Roe's finest ever work
in full colour – hippie mandalas and Lewis Carroll on LSD – had been
printed, as had a special full-colour edition of the *Evening Standard*,
the front cover of which boasted the image of Pete Townshend
leapfrogging a winking Rupert Bear. The poster design this year
featured a drummer boy out of *Sgt Pepper* – apparently a self-portrait
of Roe himself – with a snail at his feet and a winding road inside his
bass drum. The weekend ticket added two companions, a flute player
and guitarist with (hidden in the design) a cat, a dog, a butterfly and
psychedelic mushroom, and a human skull.

The scene was set, upwards of half a million souls were making
their way to the site. The fun-fair was pitched; let the show
commence...

Fairfield Parlour opened the first day of the Festival proper – a day
that was to spotlight the heavier sounds of contemporary rock. Music

commenced at about 2 pm and ended at 4 am the following morning with Melanie, due to have been last on the bill, fast asleep backstage.

FAIRFIELD PARLOUR

Proteges of David Symonds, they played thirty-two instruments, and impressed with a quiet, melodic performance highlighting some excellent 'folksy-contemporary numbers', though to another onlooker they sounded like 'a pastiche of Jethro Tull', breathy flute and all, and vocally they were unbelievably twee. There were reasons for this.

Shortly before they went on, the group were told that there had been an anonymous letter – presumably from an irate local – threatening to shoot the first group to appear at the Festival proper. This gave an extra, underlying tension to their appearance. French anarchists were nothing to some of the militant elements already living on the Island. Admiral Sir Manley Power had earlier told friends he intended to 'shoot the scum' as they arrived; having met him and read of his record against the Japanese, this was no idle threat.

This was not the end of Fairfield Parlour's troubles. Under the name I Luv Wight, they had written and recorded an official Festival theme song, 'Let The World Wash In'. It was played once, then Rikki Farr removed it from the turntable, remarking, 'That's enough of that crap', and then threw it into the crowd like a frisbee. (Its mint value, in drummer boy sleeve, is now over £50.)

The Great Awakening's instrumental version of the hymn 'Amazing Grace' took over as official Festival theme tune. Played entirely by David Cohen of Country Joe And The Fish, a single guitar picks out the tune, then swells into an orchestra of electric guitars. 'Let The World Wash In' – like the group who played it – might well have sunk without trace, but its superb lyrics somehow prefigured the spirit of the event.

> *Ah, ah, an island is no island*
> *It is just a stepping stone.*
> *There are some things*
> *that can be done almost quietly.*
> *Let them tell you,*
> *you are for that is true.*
> *And yet you know*

We stand within a circle,
And together we shall be.

Let the world wash in,
Let it pour over and over
Daltrey/Pumer

Fairfield Parlour recorded a live album in the ballroom of the Clarendon Hotel, Shanklin; it remains unissued, and the master tapes disappeared. As Kaleidoscope – not the US band featuring David Lindley – they had been one of the first, and best, groups to purvey English psychedelia.

HAWKWIND

Meanwhile, Hawkwind and the Pink Fairies played free for the waiting crowds, on the back of an open-topped truck parked outside Canvas City. Nick Turner of Hawkwind was covered in silver paint and half naked, a sight which proved unforgettable to all those who saw him, myself included.

The Fairies drummer, the equally extraordinary Twink, had appeared with the Pretty Things at the 1969 event. David Goodman recalls:

'What we did was liberate the big inflatable tent that was behind the main stage. We basically held the guy to ransom, saying, "We're taking over. Otherwise we're going to stop the generator." So he let us in, and we had a stage, and we charged ten bob to come in and kip there.'

Hippie capitalism in action.

Perhaps the seeds of punk were sown in these rural acres. Malcolm McLaren used much the same tactics when first promoting the Sex Pistols, playing on stolen instruments, turning up unannounced and invading other bands' gigs. This kind of anarchic happening also derived from McLaren's intellectual heroes, the situationalists, some of whose slogans were daubed on the IOW fences: 'Don't buy', 'Entrance is everywhere'. Certainly Caroline Coon, later to write the first article about punk rock, was running the Release tent at the time.

ARRIVAL

Closer to pop than heavy rock, Arrival were a seven-piece band, dressed in a bizarre variety of costumes. They *arrived* in a double bladed Chinook helicopter, having just appeared at a festival in Tokyo. Arrival managed to gain the audience's attention with 'Hard Road' and sustained it with Leonard Cohen's 'Hey, That's No Way To Say Goodbye', on which Dyan Birch sang lead. After 'Sit Down And Float' (which the crowd seemed to be doing anyway) they ended with the gospel song 'See The Lord', which had almost the entire crowd on its feet, clapping, shouting and singing.

> *'Dyan Birch is a watchful Aquarian with foxy hair, and Carroll Carter is blonde and brisk and comely. Paddy McHugh is cool and thinks ahead, and Frank Collins writes songs and thinks about now.'*
> Programme note

These four harmony vocalists – like Abba doubled – later got together with the rhythm section of Joe Cocker's Grease Band, from the previous year's Festival, to form the mid-seventies band Kokomo, who more successfully united the passion of soul music with the muscle of hard rock.

LIGHTHOUSE

Next up on stage were Lighthouse, a thirteen-piece Canadian band led by drummer Skip Prokop, who staggered everyone with their instrumentation – three trumpets (one doubling mellophone), two saxes, electric piano, guitar, bass, drums, singer – and an electric string section: two violins and a solid-bodied cello. They stretched out in a single line right across the stage, with the brass to the left of the stage, the rhythm in the centre and the string section to the right.

Starting with 'Hey Jude', their update of 'Give Peace A Chance' had everybody standing up, arms upraised in a forest of peace signs. They played expanded versions of the Byrds' 'Eight Miles High', and the Band's 'Chest Fever', which began with ear-splitting riffs, like the title sequence of a Hollywood movie, and featured Prokop's 'mind-shattering drumming'. Like Arrival before them, they boasted unusually fine vocal harmonies, especially on their last number, a medley of rock standards, 'Let's Stand Together'. The sort of band made for large open air festivals; you would never see the likes of Lighthouse at your down town rock club!

Lighthouse were so well received that they were immediately asked to reappear the following day to perform an extended Beatles medley, and popped up on stage whenever another band had gone missing. Their cause was not hindered by the identity of their manager – Rikki Farr.

'Everybody seemed to be brought together by the music; this is what festivals are about. Unfortunately, such moments are rare.'

TASTE

Rikki Farr next announced, 'Three great musicians – TASTE!' The applause was deafening. A band with a huge cult following, all of whom appeared to be at the Festival. The sun was coming down in the late afternoon and the mood and temperature was just right. Starting with 'What's Going On', they ran through their set to undiminished adulation. 'Sugar Mama' went down well, as did 'Gambling Blues', with Gallagher on bottleneck guitar, and 'Sinner Boy', as captured on film by Murray Lerner. Gallagher showed his ability – like Alvin Lee – to play long passages at high speed. He had the photographers working overtime.

'Taste really is Rory Gallagher, swaying back and forth, hair flying and mouth open in apparent ecstasy at finding note sequences maybe even HE didn't think possible. Sometimes he makes it look so easy, just standing there and ripping the notes out. At others he bends almost double, sways and leaps around like a man possessed.'

Called back for an encore, Rory launched into a musical battle with drummer John Wilson and then bassist Richie McCracken, which involved his playing a line and letting the other musicians copy it. This started with simple runs, then progressed (literally) to very complicated musical structures. Taste left the stage, only to return twice more, setting the atmosphere alight with 'Same Old Story'. The roars that continued for long after they were gone were deafening and it's certain that, had time and energy allowed, Taste would have played all afternoon and well into the night.

Taste had just played an all-nighter at the Lyceum, where most of their gear had been stolen after the gig, so John Wilson 'had to run around like mad scrounging a bass pedal from here, a cymbal from there until I could made up a complete drum kit'. The bassist remembers it being a very intense gig, 'probably because the band had already decided to split up'.

Just when they seemed about to break through into mass acceptance, though, Taste broke up. Rory Gallagher's solo career never quite reached the same heights, and when he died in the summer of 1995, he was remembered not just for his innate modesty and ability, but for a talent never quite fulfilled. Gallagher was far more than a simple recycler of blues riffs, as tributes from many Irish traditional musicians – and from Dylan and Van Morrison – amply testify. The LP *Taste Live At The Isle Of Wight*, released in 1971, is an interesting document of what turned out to be the band's last ride. Gallagher's songs 'What's Going On', 'Sugar Mama', 'Morning Sun' and 'Sinner Boy' are augmented with Big Bill Broonzy's 'Feel So Good' and the traditional blues 'Catfish'. The cover shot is similarly evocative.

Next on the menu was an unscheduled dialogue between Rikki Farr and an American gentleman who had been screaming ruderies from the arena. Farr invited him to the microphone to air his grievances to the multitude, and the American complied by bemoaning the commercial rip-off aspects to the Festival (that is, having to pay to get in) and also the presence of police dogs inside the spectator area. 'This a psychedelic concentration camp.' Farr answered such charges in his best cooling-down-the masses tone, and ended by demanding that all dogs depart from the arena. He should have become a politician!

TONY JOE WHITE
A cool and unflappable customer who appeared in the early evening just after an angry section of the crowd had voiced its disapproval of the ten guinea VIP enclosure – which fronted the stage – by lobbing coke cans and other missiles in its direction. The audience quickly warmed to the large, beaming, calm man from the Deep South.

He kicked off with John Lee Hooker's 'Boom Boom' getting an amazing sound from simple guitar, using wah-wah pedal and vibrato, and backed only by Cozy Powell – borrowed from Jeff Beck's group for the occasion – on drums. Together they created a mood of quiet, understated funkiness. Songs like 'Polk Salad Annie', 'Want You', 'Roosevelt And Ira Lee', and the inevitable 'Groupie Girl' were blessed with dollops of down-home guitar and cool, drawling vocals, and Tony Joe's introductions were highly entertaining.

He didn't seem to be put off his stroke, either, when interrupted by a gentleman who apparently had a spontaneous desire to commend the altruism of the organisers over the public address system, merely commenting, 'Y'all seem tuh be havin' an election over here!' Probably the least appreciated act of the whole Festival, Tony Joe's act was full of warmth, charm and humour.

CHICAGO

Introduced as America's greatest group – which must have been news to the Doors, the Airplane, the Grateful Dead, the Beach Boys, the Band, the Velvet Underground... *Message To Love* records the bullying treatment of Ray Foulk by the manager of these supposed revolutionaries due to the undersized typeface used for their name on press adverts: the Dave Roe poster is impeccably egalitarian.

'And now for your further entertainment,' blasted swinging Jeff Dexter over the PA, 'we present Chicago.' 'Huzzah, huzzah' returned the crowd as full brass, bass, guitar and everything else smacked them in the ears.

Their set began as dusk was falling. Around 8.15 pm stage lights dimmed and the mighty brass flares typical of the band fanfared their first number. The strongest impressions left by individual members were from trombonist Jim Pankow and guitarist Terry Kath, who also handled most of the vocals. His playing was fast, fluent and tough, and he looked like the kind of guy who would go down among the audience and personally sort out anyone who messed with his music. One girl actually screamed during an electrifyingly high speed guitar solo.

'Only The Beginning' from their first album – as the Chicago Transit Authority – started slowly but built to a fury. It was followed by 'I Do Love You', from their second LP, then keyboard player Robert Lamm started off 'Does Anybody Know What Time It Really Is' with a free-form solo before the others took up the tune and funked it up. 'Mother', an early diatribe against pollution, featured Walt Parazaider's flute, which was a joy. Some thought the arrangements were 'no more adventurous or novel than any good Stax session', which underrates Stax, but mass excitement – and a huge ovation – finally came with '25 Or 6 To 4' and the encore, 'I'm A Man'. 'That's it – you're too much. You're beautiful. We're gonna split,' said the laconic but pleased Mr Kath.

Walt Parazaider remembers buying a jacket in Carnaby Street the previous day, only to find that trombonist Jimmy Pankow had bought an identical jacket, so both ended up wearing the same clothes on stage.

It seems strange to have the day's bill toppers half way through the evening, but it was an inspired piece of timing. It was only their second appearance in Britain – after one night at the Royal Albert Hall – and they would have brought the roof down, if there had been a roof to bring down, not the clear night skies of Afton.

> *'Chicago believe that in order to progress musically there must be regular development individually as well as in the unit. They adhere to a strict rehearsal schedule, hold writing seminars and gather often for discussions relating to performance and material. They are also united within a social framework. The members of Chicago have been together for years and so it is a family as well as a work-force that has been welded.'*
> Programme note

Chicago still exist, but they have moved from being a heavily politicised, adventurous and serious big band, as outlined in the above, to being an unambitious MoR combo, churning out the occasional hit single. A metaphor for our times.

Terry Kath died in the early seventies, playing with a loaded gun.

Between Chicago and Family, Rikki Farr made another attempt to placate the Mau-Mau outside the gates by announcing that as soon as they had 170,000 paying customers inside the arena (that is, £510,000 in takings) they would declare the Festival free, because Fiery

Creations would then have broken even. He also referred to Desolation Hill.

'Did you think we were blind when we chose the site? Of course we knew what would happen, and we're breaking our agreement with the Council by not fencing the area. We will not, by any means, comply with the demand to clear the people off the hill.'

So suddenly, Uncle Rikki was on the side of the rebels, against those nasty people from the Council. Neat.

FAMILY

Family followed and Roger Chapman bleated like an entire flock of sheep driven across from Afton Farm. It was 'as if his whiskers had grown inward and he was singing through a briar patch. Chapman delivered one LONG extended croak with vibrato.' He sang 'Procession', 'A Song For Me', and the fiercely paranoid 'Drowned In Wine', with Poli Palmer demonstrating his multifarious talents on flute, electric piano and vibraphone (with and without fuzz).

They got a rousing cheer at the end – perhaps because Roger Chapman spent nearly as much time demolishing the microphone as he did singing into it – and encored with 'The Weaver's Answer', the climax of one of the best sets the band had ever played. The veins on Chapman's neck strained like whipcord as he sung 'Bad News' while John Weider and Charlie Whitney were formidable, constantly switching instruments. Rob Townsend proved one of the most thoughtful of drummers, always there to heighten the mood and add the correct punctuations.

'What makes Family a frightening band is that instead of hysteria they convey strength. If a microphone ends up in the audience, or a tambourine is splintered to matchwood it is just part of the generation of the power of the music.'
Programme note

The same line-up had played the previous festival. Family never got their due, and neither did Streetwalkers, who again featured the writing/performing team of Chapman and Whitney.

Meanwhile backstage... Roger Daltry leant over the bar while Keith Moon was constantly being sought by his relations. Granite-faced John Entwistle let loose with mock fisticuffs at a pal, and they eventually carried each other out. A very righteous young girl screamed hell and damnation at the drinkers. Falling out of her T-shirt and slightly hoarse, she meandered away...

PROCOL HARUM

Procol Harum followed Family at well past midnight, and their stately music echoed across a giant spotlight illuminating the stage, the dark bulk of 'Devastation Hill' dotted with camp fires and even a few flames inside the main arena. So that's where the lavatory doors went!

All this made the homely figure of Gary Brooker look pretty incongruous. His grand piano was properly amplified, when so many keyboard instruments in other bands had sounded distorted. Whenever the gentle and deliberate notes lulled the crowd into a sense of euphoria, then in came Robin Trower's screaming, protesting guitar. The nearest thing in sound to the Band the previous year, songs like 'Wish Me Well' and 'Conquistador' underlaid Keith Reid's enigmatic, heartfelt lyrics with the brute strength of drummer B.J. Wilson, beauty and the beat.

John Tobler remembers Trower rubbing his hands together, saying 'It's bloody cold', and playing something really rocky.

Songs from the *A Salty Dog* album brought the best reaction from the listening crowd, especially the title track – which appears on the *First Great Rock Festivals Of The Seventies* LP – with its mournful tale of shipwreck and a sailor coming home most appropriate within sound of the waves pounding the 'wreckers' coast' of the South Wight. This was also the theme of *Enoch Arden*, written just down the road.

'It's too cold to play anything slow,' said Brooker. So they launched straight into a rock 'n' roll medley closer to Jerry Lee Lewis than Alfred, Lord Tennyson, and guaranteed to get everybody going: 'Move On Down The Line', 'High School Confidential' and 'Lucille'. It left the hordes panting and unruly.

Procol Harum were – and are – a very odd combination of the restrained and the demonic. Trower went on to become a guitar hero in the Hendrix mode, but never bettered the controlled intensity of his time with the band, and they retained a firm grasp of rock 'n' roll dating back to their days as Southend rockers, The Paramounts. As the *Melody Maker* wrote:

> *'They looked weird, sounded weird and it was good to head a band with character and a strange kind of intensity.'*

The best band of the day. No one remembers if they played 'A Whiter Shade Of Pale'.

VOICES OF EAST HARLEM

Was it the Jackson Twelve? The Harlem Globetrotters? First one, then four, then eight, then seemingly dozens of bopping teenagers filed out onto the stage. They let rip with spontaneous whoops and hollers, but when the applause was sparse – as it was, for the first half-dozen numbers – they stood awkwardly, peering out through the spotlights at the assembled multitude.

It was their founder and teacher Bernice Colee, who finally fired singers and crowd alike. Dressed in a green and gold African robe and head-dress, she strutted with professional confidence in front of the kids, who added liberal verbal encouragement to her wild, unrestrained wailing on the gospel tinged 'Sing A Song Of Freedom'.

From then on it was cheering and encores all the way, particularly for eight year old Gregory, who bopped around the stage like a miniature James Brown as he sang 'Run Shaker Life'. The ideal act for 2 am, with an overall sound really filling the air, as did the roar for more when they eventually left the stage after an incredible version of John Fogerty's 'Proud Mary'.

Fifteen singers and six instrumentalists ranging in age from twelve to twenty; they all originated from New York, some from Harlem, some from the Bronx, and despite this sang of equality, freedom, peace and love. One wonders what happened to them as the great society crumbled. A difficult act to follow.

CACTUS

Cactus ended the first long day's night. The quartet of ex Vanilla Fudge rhythm section Tim Bogert and Carmine Appice, and friends Jim McCarty and Rusty Day played loud and heavy. A kind of American Led Zeppelin without the subtlety, or innate tunefulness.

'No Need To Worry' and their heavification of Mose Allison's 'Parchman Farm' appear on *The First Great Rock Festivals Of The Seventies* LP. One of those bands where the most exciting thing was the drum solo. Many doubted if Cactus said anything new, or if they were worth staying up 'til 3 am to hear. The crowd seemed to agree, for after Cactus the organisers called it a day, and Melanie good-naturedly agreed to miss a booking in Holland and play the following night.

Fatigue was followed by freezing temperatures. 'How can Cactus survive in a refrigerator like this?' one reporter asked, stumbling blind into the dark.

The whole world seemed to be making its way to Afton. One of the printers at the Foulk's Freshwater Press had to rush back to Inglefield to print more tickets. In Lymington, so much milk was sold to hippies that one milkman commented, 'I shall have to go to the Festival myself to collect the empty bottles.' Special courts were already in session to deal with drug busts, while the Royal Standard Inn in Freshwater village reported their takings had trebled.

The local hairdresser was not so lucky. 'When they see our place, they pass by on the other side of the road,' he joked. The biggest threat was to the library, when an anonymous caller threatened to break its windows because the reading room was closed for repairs. At Mottistone, the Revd Bowyer presided over a barefoot hippie wedding between a couple who had been living on the Festival site for the previous five weeks. The bride wore an orange kaftan over green corduroy slacks, the groom a black T-shirt and faded blue jeans.

No violent incidents were reported on Friday night, although work in fencing off Afton Down seemed to have faltered, and thousands were now watching the music free. Fiery Creations' main problem was a meeting with police who claimed that announcements referring to drug use had been made on stage. This probably refers to the proferred amnesty to those under seventeen who handed in their drugs. No action would be taken, Rikki Farr announced, then later he announced that precisely nobody had been tempted by the police's offer. Mass hilarity ensued.

Fiery Creations moved swiftly to announce it had issued a stern warning that anyone using drugs on stage would be immediately ejected from the site. Quite how this affected Hendrix, or Jim Morrison or Donovan has never been publicly revealed.

It was also announced that Yarmouth Castle, built by Henry VIII to repel the French, and with thick stone walls the Foulks would have killed for, was to be closed to the public. This was apparently a security measure, though against whom has never been explained.

12

Saturday 30 August, 1970

The day started late and ended later – at dawn on Sunday to be precise – with Sly And The Family Stone exalting 'I Want To Take You Higher' just before breakfast... and on very empty stomachs too.

JOHN B. SEBASTIAN

One of the veterans of Woodstock, which he described here as 'kids driving to the Revolution in their fathers' cars'. He probably saved the Festival from a complete holocaust of violence, and held the body of the crowd together. He was the only artist to turn up on Saturday morning – well after the alleged 11.30 am start – and went straight on in 'What A Day For A Daydream' type weather to appease a tense audience.

Sebastian came on after a Friday when an explosive atmosphere had built up. A lesser talent, a lesser personality might have started the day off on the wrong foot, but Sebastian could have played all day and no one would have questioned the absence of other bands.

He started with a tribute to his blonde girl friend, who had most of the photographers dividing their attention between him on stage and her in the audience, swaying and looking up at him adoringly.

No one else had arrived, so John had all the time in the world; nearly two hours to sing 'She's A Lady', 'Daydream', 'Do You Believe In Magic', 'Jug Band Music', the poignant 'Darling Be Home Soon', 'Younger Girl' and many many more.

He will be remembered as the great hit of the Isle of Wight, as Tom Paxton had been the previous year. Even events happened well for him. During one of the encores, a spray of balloons burst overhead and he incorporated the event into his song. A message arrived on the end of about half a mile of plastic tubing. He took off the white sheet and read, 'We love you'. 'Cool and beautiful,' he commented. Then he went into another monologue about Woodstock, revealing that...

'I wasn't supposed to play there even, but there was all that rain and it made electric band equipment dangerous. So they got cheap old acoustic me to fill in and let me go on and on, and I ended up one of the stars of the show and the film, I guess.'

Just at that moment, another message was passed to John, who read, 'Ask Zal on stage.' John's eyes went up two inches. 'Is Zal here?' he asked. 'Come on up,' John invited and bearded Zal leapt onto the stage, and they hugged each other a lot. It was the first reuniting of the former Lovin' Spoonful stars after three years. Zal grabbed a guitar and they both went into 'Blues In The Bottle'. Then John sang a song called 'Boredom', written in a Dayton, Ohio holiday inn, and then Zal took over to sing a happy song about 'Bald Headed Lena', and then John sang again, and came back with a torrid bit of harmonica soloing as an encore to a great act.

Finally, after 140 gloriously unforgettable minutes, he waved his way off stage having exhausted himself and his repertoire. For the rest of the Festival, Zal Yanovsky was ubiquitous, he became a symbol of permanence; he was there on his feet to applaud Joni Mitchell singing 'Woodstock', he was there outside the refreshment tent with a bottle of Teachers talking to anybody and everybody. He was there all the time, and you felt that if he was there, somewhere, the Festival would go on, and that if he went away, it would collapse.

SHAWN PHILIPS

Philips, in glasses, was lanky with long blonde hair in a ponytail, and the aura of a world-travelled Texan. Unbilled, he proved a good acoustic guitarist and singer of his own songs, like 'Old Covered Wagon', 'Hey Miss Lonely', and other numbers from his current LP. He was a friend of Donovan, which is why he was at the Festival, and presumably he offered to fill in.

LIGHTHOUSE

They made a second appearance, and built up to a fine climax with a peace medley of 'Hey Joe', 'Give Peace A Chance' and 'All You Need Is Love'.

MUNGO JERRY

'Goodtime jugthumping music', the programme note said, and thus ideal for the afternoon shift. Although Mungo Jerry were present on site they did not actually play, so we were denied the sight of Ray Dorset's mutton chop sideburns, or his boots stomping in time with the music. 'In The Summertime' did get lots of plays over the PA, though.

Ray Dorset:

'We came down from Edinburgh by car, a new Ford Capri. I remember Roger Daltrey on the ferry with his DB5 Aston Martin. We got frisked by plain clothes policeman looking like hippies. The only thing was that they hadn't grown their hair long. It was a bit like Benny Hill.'

Mungo Jerry were asked to go on late on Friday night, but they were tired and so were the audience, and then they were bombarded by the press. They had to leave on Saturday for a gig in Venice, and then immediately begin an American tour.

Freek Press, under the eye-catching headline 'Watch these fuzz' identified the plain clothes officers, including 'a cop couple in their late twenties. Him: sleeveless afghan jacket, short dark hair like a skull cap. Her: mousy, shoulder length hair, oval face.' Perhaps easier to spot was the subject of a special warning. 'Be extra careful of Bailey from Ryde... a mafia gangster, wide grin, long sideburns and a 3d straw hat.' Or perhaps he was just on holiday.

JONI MITCHELL

Farr announced, 'A lovely surprise for you – Joni Mitchell' and on she walked, diffident yet majestic in a long yellow dress, and obviously nervous about performing alone to such a huge crowd. The atmosphere was good, nurtured by Sebastian and the crowd were relaxing in the summer sun, but half way through 'Chelsea Morning' she stopped, declared, 'I don't feel like singing that song very much', moved over to the piano, and announced that she'd sing 'Woodstock'.

Suddenly, with terrifying swiftness, the vibes turned right around. A man in the VIP area, twenty-five yards from the stage, cried, 'Help... we need a doctor', and all eyes swung towards a swaying, puppet-like figure obviously on the worst of bad trips. In an instant the stage was full of frightened eyes and everyone was standing, staring at the ghastly figure, who was resisting attempts to drag him away. Joni went back to the piano stool, picked out the opening chords of 'Woodstock' and began the song. She could not have made a worse choice. At that moment, with brief terror in the air, we were anything but stardust and golden, and the garden had become a place of squalor. She announced:

'This is a song about another festival. I didn't actually go there, I only got as far as New York airport, but I saw it all on television and wrote a song about it.'

The atmosphere settled slightly, but was still charged with tension when suddenly a small bearded American, chillingly reminiscent of Charles Manson, seized the microphone and started to recite 'a very important message for the people of Devastation Hill'. This, with total irony, brought to an abrupt halt 'For Free', her song about a London busker. He was not allowed to continue, as the stagehands and Joni's retinue pinioned his arms and forced him off, and the crowd began to bay 'Let him speak... let him speak'. That privilege is afforded to those

138

who watch Murray Lerner's film, and what the audience missed is a stoned rant about arranging to meet with Joni on stage.

Joni, shaken and in tears, composed herself, then made a telling speech, about the relationship between art and life, about how she puts her whole being into her music, and expects the same from an audience, not (it is implied) a near death experience.

> *'Last Sunday, I went to a Hopi Indian ceremony, where some of the Indians were behaving like Indians and some of the Indians were behaving like tourists. I think you're behaving like tourists, man ... give us some respect!'*

She sang again, and lightened the atmosphere with a love-song to Graham Nash, and 'California', her ballad about homesickness, on which she played dulcimer. One line, *'We asked for peace but they didn't give us a chance'*, was particularly apt. She was called back for four encores – including a supercharged 'Big Yellow Taxi' – which in Lerner's film follows straight on – and 'Both Sides Now'. By the time she finally left the stage, she had defused a potentially dangerous situation, simply through the sheer beauty of her songs. The ovation which greeted her final item was tremendous, almost as if the multitude was offering an apology for the misbehaviour of an unwelcome minority.

Undoubtedly the most emotional performance of the weekend. An early and major influence on Fairport Convention, who helped popularise her songs, she later moved closer to modern jazz, and even world music. Neil Young was set to appear backing her on guitar, but he turned his vintage Rolls-Royce back at Yarmouth after his manager had been busted for drugs.

> *'Her voice and her acoustic guitar are free, pure instruments in themselves; there is an additional beauty in the way she uses them to convey such a full range of idea-emotions. But if she looked like your grandmother and her voice cracked and she only knew three chords, her performance would be justified by the songs alone.'*

Programme note

TINY TIM

Backstage in 1969, the psychedelic artist Martin Sharp, dressed as a harlequin, told Richard Neville:

> *'If only Tiny Tim was here... he's the one who can link up all the generations, a true minstrel of the age, ambiguous, multi-voiced, an immortal innocent, the most incredible songbird in captivity.'*

Conversely, *Message To Love* juxtaposes Tim trilling that all music should be free, with an agent's bitter comment that Tiny wouldn't even tune his ukulele without $25,000 in cash upfront.

The immortal Mr Herbert Khaury, alias Tiny Tim, alias Larry Love the Singing Canary, probably only popular still because his appearances are so rare, arrived with his ukulele, held it above his head in triumph, blew the expected kisses and launched into his selection of music hall favourites that were hits between 1915 and 1930, without giving the militants a chance to protest.

That over, and the initial impact of seeing this incredible man again having sunk in, it promised to be boring. Then, amazingly, he broke into John Fogerty's 'Proud Mary' with all the hip movements of a 1950's rock star. 'Blue Suede Shoes' followed on 'Rock Around The Clock' and 'Great Balls Of Fire', midway through which he did a Tom Jones by removing his tie and throwing it into the crowd.

His rock 'n' roll medley featured some of the most untogether playing ever heard: 'This is my wonderful English band... my wonderful English band,' he trilled with New York sarcasm. They included two local musicians, Jack Richards on drums – ex Perception and the Mel Taylor Four – and Cas Caswell on bass. It is only fair to point out that they were given very little notice of what was expected of them, and they appeared on stage without any previous rehearsal. Then it was time for Tiny to hoist his megaphone. Through it he warbled those patriotic favourites 'The White Cliffs Of Dover', 'There'll Always Be An England' and 'Land Of Hope And Glory', which brought an unexpectedly ecstatic reaction. Lerner's film pans across a field full of folk flashing the 'peace' sign in time to the music. One can only imagine with a shudder the reaction today. The peace signs might even be reversed.

'Isle of Wight tomatoes are wonderful,' said Tiny Tim as he tiptoed off on the arm of Miss Vicky. He must have made a really big impression on one particular guy in the audience – maybe Martin Sharp was back – because at various intervals throughout the remainder of the event, he was to be heard calling loudly for the return of his idol.

> *'I sang in hospitals and for the poor in the streets. I even sang in back alleys and in subway trains, just to sing whatever the people wanted to hear. All I wanted to do was to spread joy all over. I always bring my little ukulele along in my shopping bag which my dear sweet father bought me.*
>
> *'The spirits of the singers whose songs I do are living within me. That's why the songs come out in the voices of the original singers. I'm not doing imitations. Why do I do a lot of things in falsetto? For me that voice is all happiness and sunshine... it is the light, youthful, gay, romantic spirit of my heart.'*

Programme note

Meanwhile back on the beach... thousands of sightseers went to Compton Bay during the Festival to watch the hippies bathing nude. At least 500 people in varying states of undress were on the beach that afternoon enjoying the sun, the sea, some were even making sand castles, but above all they were enjoying themselves. They sang to guitars, someone was beating a bongo and then from the top of the steps came the jingle of a tambourine, as if summoned by Bob Dylan from the previous year.

The tambourine man was singing, imploring more of them to take off their clothes, get rid of their hang-ups. They responded and soon the whole beach seemed to be rocking in time with the beat of his tambourine and the clapping hands. They crowded round the tambourine man and some began to dance and sing wildly. 'Let's go in the sea, let's go in the sea,' he cried and like a latter day Pied Piper he led his hippie band to the water. A giant circle was formed and they began singing, 'We *shall* overcome. *Please* give peace a chance.' And they meant it.

All over the site, the interval between Tiny Tim and Miles Davis was euphoric as all present stood, danced and sang along with Otis

Redding's 'Respect' and Free's 'All Right Now'. During the latter, a technicolour hot air balloon carrying two intrepid aviators appeared over the site, and received maybe half a million two-handed peace signs. A nice moment.

MILES DAVIS

Miles took the stage in a red leather jacket and silver-studded jeans and boots, at forty-four years old as hip as any there. His first morse code notes played out as dusk was coming in and the first campfires flickered on the side of the mountain. In his band were Gary Bartz (alto and soprano saxes), Chick Corea (organ), Keith Jarrett (electric piano), Dave Holland (bass), Jack DeJohnette (drums) and Airto Moreira (percussion).

The group's use of rock rhythms was far more evident than before, but they proved beyond any doubt that they were capable of making it as subtle, as complex, and as rewarding as any conventional jazz rhythm. Holland laid down a fragmented but solid bass line, and Miles blew brief, jabbing solos over the massively shifting backdrop. Corea and Jarrett, despite being handicapped by inferior borrowed instruments, weaved textures of unerring subtlety and rightness, and the band left after more than an hour to an ovation.

Murray Lerner's film captures the excitement of the music as it happened, with Miles majestic and silhouetted against the sky. When he was asked what this piece was to be called, when part of it appeared on the the *First Great Rock Festivals Of The Seventies* LP, he said, 'Call it anythin'.' And thus it was named.

TEN YEARS AFTER

They started with 'Love Like A Man', 'Good Morning Little Schoolgirl' and a very long and excessively noisy 'No Title'. As at Woodstock, they brought the house down with their rock 'n' roll medley 'I'm Going Home', followed by 'Sweet Little Sixteen'. Rarely have they played better. One Frenchman was so moved by 'Love Like A Man' that he stripped naked and tried to clamber on the stage.

The famous Alvin Lee–Leo Lyons confrontation took place during the 'wicked' 'Good Morning Little Schoolgirl'. This involved the two guitarists standing about a foot apart facing one another as if in unarmed combat. Chick Churchill's organ was as usual almost lost among the wall of sound but he came into his own during 'No Time', Ric Lee having played a great 'half a drum solo' on the preceding number, 'Hobbit'.

As TYA launched into 'I'm Going Home', which had by now become their anthem, the crowd rose to its feet and began clapping and cheering as one. Alvin tore into the number, contorting his face like a man in terminal pain, his fingers a blur as he simultaneously played at break-neck speed and screamed the lyrics into the mike, including a snatch of 'Blue Suede Shoes' along the way. *Rolling Stone* described Lee as 'Frankie Avalon on acid' purveying 'saucy savagery' and a simulation of oral sex. And I thought he was just a white bluesman!

A good entertaining band, but maybe because of such hyperbole – or plain hype – they soon became little more than a vehicle for Lee's fast but shallow solos. Early sessions for John Peel had shown a jazzier side to the band with tracks like 'At The Woodchoppers Ball', which they failed to develop.

They reformed in 1978 as Ten Years Later, which drew attention to their rock 'n' roll roots: like the Beatles, they trained on the Hamburg circuit, playing three sets a night. On the *First Great Rock Festivals Of The Seventies* TYA play 'I Can't Keep From Cryin' Sometimes', and they also appear in supercharged form in Murray Lerner's film. The recent Radio 1 Festival documentary featured the live version of 'Going Home', a quarter of an hour of excitement and dynamics, which has actually improved with age.

Gary Brooker recalls that TYA were sharing a rented mansion with two other Chrysalis bands, Jethro Tull and his own band Procol Harum.

'When we finished our set, Chick Churchill came back with us although the rest of his band had gone straight back to London. He pretended to have lost his wallet. Truth was, he'd fallen for the landlord's daughter, Suzanne, and wanted the excuse to hang around her a bit longer. In the end they got married and they stayed married for twenty five years.'

Ian Anderson had less pleasant memories of the same house.

*'I woke up in extreme terror because something seemed to be
sitting on my chest. It was pressing me down on the bed and
then, suddenly, it just moved away and was gone. There were
also beds and furniture moving about in the night. The
landlord said it was a poltergeist.'*

Perhaps it was just Chick Churchill and Suzanne, getting to know one
another.

EMERSON, LAKE AND PALMER

Making their debut in front of a large audience – they had played one
warm up gig – this new supergroup were inevitably somewhat ill-
rehearsed. Keith Emerson was his usual flamboyant self, twenty year
old Carl Palmer drummed with express-train energy and flash, and
Greg Lake pinned it together on bass and vocals, but it still didn't quite
gel.

Emerson played two Hammond organs at the same time during the
opening number, 'Barbarian', then things calmed down for 'Take A
Pebble' with Greg on acoustic guitar. A forty-minute version of *Pictures
At An Exhibition* was musically brilliant and featured the keyboard
maestro playing Moog synthesiser and setting off two small cannons on
stage, blowing off the glasses of a spectator sitting in the firing line.

People were yelling for 'America' and 'She Belongs To Me' under the
impression that they were listening to the Nice. That was last year.
What they got was a version of 'Rondo' that wasn't a patch on
Emerson's previous band, more of a drum showcase. They finished
with a rock 'n' roll instrumental, B. Bumble and the Stingers' 'Nut
Rocker', which came too late to really get the crowd going.

ELP were a precursor of glitter rock; wearing shining combinations
of leather and lamé, with Emerson modelling a silver-blue superstar
suit – in Lerner's film it looks more like kitchen foil – and shoving briar
pipes into his organ keys. Their use of a £3,000 prototype Moog
synthesiser prefigured the technological advance that would eventually
do for guitar rock, at least for most of the eighties, by which token ELP
were the most progressive band on the entire bill.

Not altogether to my own taste, but as Chris Welch pointed out with
a pinch or two of irony:

'Despite the mutterings of the underground press, there were one or two people who enjoyed them. There was, for instance, some guy at the back of the crowd, who managed to make his voice sound like several thousand people cheering!'

THE DOORS

At five minutes past midnight, the Doors shambled on stage. Despite contemporary reports to the contrary, I found them magnificent, with Morrison's voice coming over clear and passionate. Lerner's film, and the Radio 1 material bears out quite how superb they were.

The Doors sneaked out on stage and everybody in the world stood up. Everybody else behind them threw beer cans until they sat down. A bearded Morrison was content to stand stock still and deliver his sombre songs while organist Ray Manzarek, guitarist Robbie Krieger and drummer John Densmore provided an equally sinister backing.

Morrison was almost unrecognisable from the young Adonis on the Electra LP covers: he was now heavily bearded with long tousled hair and wearing an embroidered black coat, like an angel of death. He grasped onto the microphone, keeping himself upright after thirty-six hours without sleep, and proceeded to sing his heart out. They opened with 'Backdoor Man', then smoothly segued into 'Break On Through' and a tumultuous 'When The Music's Over'. The mysterious 'Ship Of Fools', from *Morrison Hotel* was slowed down to a lament, then 'Light My Fire' was the signal for hundreds of small fires to be lit in the arena. They finished with an epic version of 'The End', with Morrison improvising a long section from his poem 'Celebration Of The Lizard' half way through. As Sue Fellies remembers, the scream at the end of the line *'We want the world and we want it NOW'* was truly agonising, as through it he gave vent to all his frustrations and sorrows. Radio 1 recently broadcast the IOW performance of 'The End', shorn of its oedipal closing monologue, but ominous to the point of nightmare.

Backstage, Morrison was at the bar, bewhiskered and looking like a lumberjack, preoccupied with his Miami court case on the charge of exposure. A bra-less wench, starstruck, blurted, 'You mean if you did it in New York you'd just get a fast fine and that's all?'

'I didn't do it anywhere,' replied Morrison with distaste.

'It's no longer a joke,' added Ray.

'We can talk about it over here, but we couldn't in the States. He is up on at least four charges and they are out for his blood – they want to hang him. If he's convicted of exposure, he could get get over two years in a place called Rayfer's Jail and that's a southern swamp jail – he'd literally be on a chain gang.

'I was up on stage, and he didn't do it. True, Jim's act is foul and lewd, but he knew not to go that far, and he didn't. This couldn't have happened anywhere else in the country, but the people in the South need some time yet to come round. The kids are alright, but the other people haven't got over the Confederate scene in the Civil War. At a toll booth down there, my wife and I met the prototypes of the "Easy Rider" characters coming the opposite way in a truck. They had shotguns and the whole lot.'

The Doors' performance took place in semi-darkness, more of a religious ceremony than just another gig. There was a sense of danger in the air, the idea that doors could be opened onto some previously unknown level of existence. Within a year, Morrison was dead – or, some people claim, not – his grave in Paris an object of twisted veneration.

Oliver Stone's movie *The Doors*, starring Val Kilmer as a visually perfect Morrison, has only intensified interest in the life and work of a man who combined sex, poetry, and drugs – half shaman, half sham – into a unique alchemy. Ian Curtis of Joy Division was one of many singers who followed in his footsteps, but one of the few to capture the same scary reality, of balancing on the edge.

Morrison was the only artist to contribute to a fund set up for fans unfortunate enough to be busted for drugs possession.

Like Hendrix, Janis Joplin and Brian Jones, Morrison was himself set on a course of self-destruction from the very start. The process was deeply affecting, if you didn't yourself have to live by it.

'The DOORS are Here. And the DOORS are Now. We want the world; and we want you to have it too. NOW.'
Programme note

THE WHO

'And now – a nice rock band from Shepherds Bush – the "Oo",' said Jeff Dexter, and one of the great groups of our time ran on stage. Pete Townshend immediately cheered up English fans who had listened in silence all day to the bleatings of European and US politicos by saying, 'We come 'ome and find ourselves playing to a load of fuckin' foreigners causing trouble.' He was only kidding, but we knew what he meant.

John Entwistle stood stock-still and stone faced, his clothes painted like a skeleton, while Townshend modelled an off-the-peg boiler suit and Roger Daltrey was in his customary tassles. Keith Moon was... Keith Moon.

They must have played for three, maybe four hours. They started about one o'clock on Sunday morning, and by the time they were finished it was nearly dawn. The Who's performance was the high spot of the Festival for most people. Beginning with 'I Can't Explain', Daltrey excelled himself on 'Young Man Blues' and a new song 'Water' – *'I need me water, and maybe someone's daughter'*. Moon hurled a stick on high and then caught it, to a burst of spontaneous applause.

There was a certain amount of bated breath as to whether they would produce some major new work. But as the humorous by-play between the drummer and guitarist indicated, we were going to get the old war-horse unleashed. They did a whole chunk of *Tommy*, up to the magical *'See me, feel me, touch me, heal me'* chorus of 'We Ain't Gonna Take It'.

The Who played on well after 4 am and at quarter past four came a thrilling moment when they turned huge spotlights onto the crowd from back stage, lighting up the masses, including a flurry of moths, leaping like loons in the vastness. Pete leapt – a few others can play guitar as well, but none who can leap through the air at the same time – and Roger twirled as the band ground into 'Shaking All Over', 'Summertime Blues' and a virtual reprise of the *Live At Leeds* LP. At 4.25 am they led into 'Substitute' with no sign of tiring, and getting on for 5 am their battle hymn 'My Generation' should have been the last number.

Here Pete made a tactical error and carried on into 'Magic Bus', which was never their best song. Nevertheless, the Who's marathon was one of the most enjoyable segments amidst the mass of magic. They sounded superb, not least because their own speakers were used to boost the Festival's sound system. Townshend's mike was turned up louder than Daltrey's; they played much the same set as they had at Wootton and Woodstock in 1969, but longer! As Rod Allen wrote:

> *'There's something about the Who, the mad, demonic Who, which gets under your skin and into your head, your heart and your body.'*

As Murray Lerner's film shows, this was perhaps their finest ever performance.

MELANIE
She broke the dawn chorus with a charming selection of songs from her first two albums. Little innocent Melanie, the Shirley Temple of folk music, perhaps should not have been out so late – but she sat and whispered through songs like 'Mr Tambourine Man' and 'Ruby Tuesday'.

Melanie was obviously deeply touched by her reception. She was introduced by Keith Moon, and after she'd left the stage, Andy Dunkley the DJ played 'She's A Lady' for her.

It was 6.30 am, and dawn light was beginning to illumine the stage. Bags had grown under the eyes of all those still awake. Sleepers crashed out on a soggy bed of half-eaten hamburgers, coke tins and soup cups, immune to the constant bellow from the giant speakers. On stage, a new set of amplifiers and glistening instruments was being put together by what looked like a team of movie set designers. It heralded America's gaudiest group, and they were gaudy right down to their amp knobs.

SLY AND THE FAMILY STONE
Overbooking of acts had produced such a pile-up that the splendiferous Sly And The Family Stone, coloured hankies secured to their Afros, only got to go on at 6.30 in the fish-grey morning. Their

music was so unbelievably happy, they really made it a nice morning. When Sly walked on stage with the Family Stone, he looked like Niagra Falls on feet. He flowed and seeped across the floor in thick fur boots, tassles made of heavy beads, sunglasses and a white hat topped with a feather.

Their brass was excellent, the singing good and the only set back was Sly's bad guitar playing. When he stuck to organ it was fine. Numbers like 'Stand!' show why such a mysterious mythology had built up around them. They trooped on, minus Sister Rose who had missed the plane, for what amounted to little more than a rehearsal. Tuning up after their first number, they got it on with 'Stand!', but the exhausted audience mostly stayed sitting down. After forty-five minutes, they gave up, and left the stage following an announcement that the arena had to be cleared and cleaned up. Booing erupted, and an empty can bounced off Brother Freddy's guitar.

Sly promised to return on Sunday night. He didn't. As a DJ and producer, he was in at the start of the San Franciscan music explosion, and his own effect on black psychedelic soul – the likes of George Clinton, Bootsy Collins, even Prince – was incalculable.

Sly Stone himself descended into a drug-fuelled decline, from which he has not emerged. Jeff Dexter remembers that after the set the band stayed around in a caravan at the back of the stage, and 'kept partying with loads of cocaine. They didn't want to go home.'

Two songs, 'Stand!' and 'You Can Make It If You Try', appear on the *First Great Rock Festivals Of The Seventies* LP.

It was now undoubtedly morning, but the audience was refusing – or too tired – to leave the arena so that it could be prepared for the next day's entertainment. The kids refused to go, and so Rikki Farr asked Joni Mitchell to cool them out. It seemed a long time since her own performance, which had been part of the same day's programme! Joni talked about how beautiful everyone was, how she loved them all and how everyone was behaving like children, 'What do you want to do – start a war?'. After a volley of coke cans had rained down around her head the kids did cool down – though they still refused to go.

Eventually Fiery Creations capitulated. They let the audience stay, after making them burn their tickets to stop people going out with a handful to get others in free.

13

Sunday 31 August, 1970

S unday morning saw thousands of bleak faces, punch drunk with tiredness. The nests of hair were tangled from days of damp, chilling wind, but sleeping-bagged rompers were dauntless. The applause and requests for encores continued, act after act after act. The bill had been drawn up, scrapped and redrawn countless times as some artists played for hours on end, delaying later appearances. The ground was an obstacle course of beer cans, cups, paper and colourful garbage of all sorts mixed with rich brown mud.

GOOD NEWS
They opened proceedings, according to one report. An acoustic duo from America, with Larry Gold on cello and Michael Bacon on guitar.

> *'They recently completed the scores for two plays in their native Philadelphia – one for the Theatre of Living Arts and the other for incidental music in Michael McClure's Gargoyle, in which they not only wrote and scored but also performed.'*
> Programme note

KRIS KRISTOFFERSON

He was virtually booed off stage again, but went down slightly better this time, largely because he was joined by Zal Yanovsky. On bass was Billy Swan, who later had a hit single with the souped-up rockabilly of 'I Can Help'. Kristofferson, who angrily walks off at the end of 'Me And Bobby McGee' in Murray Lerner's film, later blamed his reception on the fact that his group had only one rehearsal, in his hotel before the concert.

One of the pioneers of the 'new country', he attracted only derision at Afton. 'Who *is* this guy,' one witness plaintively asked. Well, he had traipsed to Peru with Dennis Hopper to write the soundtrack for *The Last Movie* and later himself became a film star, acting with Dylan in Peckinpah's *Pat Garrett And Billy The Kid*.

RALPH MCTELL

Despite his self-confessed nervousness, McTell was as melodic and as dextrous as ever. As soon as his feet touched the stool's cross-bar he accelerated into Blind Boy Fuller's 'Truckin' Little Baby'. His song of school days, 'Chalk Dust' was well received, as was his ballad about loneliness in the Metropolis, 'Streets Of London', already a folk standard.

He began as a ragtime guitar player. The vocals came later, as did the songwriting.

'I don't deliberately set out to do anything through music or song. Just like anybody else I respond and react to whatever mood or situation I'm in. I'm hit from all sides by all sorts of things, things that seem sad, bad, funny, wonderful, futile, powerful – some of these things stay with me. They seem to take me over and occupy my mind until I'm forced to give them an expression. When a theme of mood develops like this, I can sometimes concentrate for weeks trying to decide which of two incredibly simple words is right for what has to be said. The melody, or at least the way I play it, takes hundreds of performances to reach a settled form – if it ever does.'
Programme note

McTell remembers: 'I stayed in a great big hotel with a Victorian dining room with Sly And The Family Stone. Sly came down to breakfast in his stage gear, unless you normally wear a purple hat at breakfast.'

HEAVEN

Jazz–rock from Portsmouth, just across the water. They were discovered by Rikki Farr, who signed them to CBS. With a line-up of two guitars, trumpet, drums, soprano and tenor sax, they were an English version of Chicago, but heavier. They recorded a double album, in an elaborate fold out sleeve, and then disappeared.

During the act, a gigantic orange balloon filled with hydrogen broke loose from its mooring and rolled round in front of the stage area and out into the audience, causing amusement to the fans but consternation to the officials as it bumped into the power cables, bringing heaven or hell nearer! Heaven played on regardless, and won over a largely apathetic crowd who were waiting for bigger names to appear.

FREE

'If Maria Callas ever wants coaching in dramatic gestures, she need go no further than Free's singer, Paul Rodgers, who carries on like Marcel Marceau with words. And Paul Kossoff, good lead guitarist that he is, earned the nickname "The Human Flycatcher" because his mouth was rarely less than wide open.'

That was one view of Free's best ever live performance. They had played much the same set in 1969, but by now had hit their stride as a band which combined the musical strengths of an 'underground' blues band with the songwriting abilities and visual excitement of the finest pop music.

'Pony' was followed by 'Woman' and then 'The Stealer', played live for the first time. 'Fire And Water' led into 'The Hunter', with an excellent, screaming solo from Kossoff. On 'I'm A Mover', bassist Andy

Fraser rocked from side to side, his instrument almost a second lead guitar, while Simon Kirke on drums anchored the sound and kept it as tight as the proverbial duck's arse. Their hit single 'All Right Now' went down well, and the band encored on Robert Johnson's 'Crossroads', which pleased Cream fans in the audience.

Three tracks from a later Island video – 'All Right Now', 'Mr Big' and 'Be My Friend' – represented some of the first footage to be commercially released from Murray Lerner's IOW Festival film. Free are captured forever with a backdrop of a psychedelic light show behind, and the huge audience in front. It is easy to see the VIP enclosure in front of the stage, with metal seats, and then the mass of humanity behind. In their first number, Kossoff's solo is played over aerial film of the Festival, the camp site and the downs. Spectacular stuff.

> *'FREE music is/free of categories,/free of labels,/free of neat pigeonholes./Basically it's blues,/but FREE are fine musicians/ and have moved away enough/from the roots for that tag/to be totally inadequate. It's FREE,/that's what it is.'*
> Programme note

Free split up in the early 1970s, but then reformed with Tetsu on bass. Andy Fraser, the musical heartbeat of the group, went off to form Sharks. Paul Kossoff, increasingly ravaged by drug dependency, left to form Back Street Crawler, but died in 1975 of a heart attack. His father, the actor and raconteur David Kossoff, toured the country telling his son's story in an attempt to stop other youngsters getting hooked on drugs.

Rodgers and Kirke later formed Bad Company.

It was just after Free – ironically – had left the stage, at about 4 pm that Rikki Farr made a dramatic announcement.

> *'This Festival cannot ever break even, so we're going to make it free as from this minute. Open the gates, and for God's sake let's have some music.'*

The crowd erupted. They sang 'Swing Low' and 'Give Peace A Chance'. And they threw the peace sign high in the air.

DONOVAN

The first 'free' music was provided by Donovan, who arrived on stage armed only with an acoustic guitar. He opened with 'Catch The Wind', the song that brought him to fame, in which he now missed off the final consonants of each word, thus obtaining a vaguely Marc Bolan-ish effect. Back to 1968, and Godshill!

Donovan was dressed in a gypsy waistcoat, white shirt and white pants inside knee-length black boots, with a harmonica fixed in front of his mouth on a wire, just like the young Bob Dylan. In his soft, wavery, watery voice, he charmed the crowd with a long minstrel tale of 'Three Brothers' and of merry men drowned in the sea. Another ocean tale, 'Sailing Homeward', was sung with genuine pathos. Next came a novelty song, 'How Much Of A Pee Do You Wee When You're Little And Only Three', with a chorus line of three small blonde boys (some reckoned they were girls), which had Joan Baez laughing backstage, and then 'Hurdy Gurdy Man', though he couldn't persuade the audience to join in. A nursery song about an old woman who swallowed a fly, and so on, amused, and took many of us back to Uncle Mac and *Children's Hour.*

After the mysterious 'Atlantis', he picked up an electric guitar for only the second time in public, the first being at the Bath Festival. Donovan now 'rocked out' with two other musicians: Mike Thomson on bass and twelve string, and bongo player John Carr. Leading off with 'First There Is A Mountain', they played a tight set which included 'Train Whistle Blues', 'Season Of The Witch', 'Mellow Yellow', and the controversial 'Poke At The Pope'. He later commented:

> *'When you're on your own, and you're used to a concert setting, it's difficult with all those people. I thought it got better when Mike and John joined me – it was more complete then.'*

Donovan would have re-enacted his 'saviour' role of Bath had John Sebastian not already done so a day earlier. A good, but overlong set.

PENTANGLE

Veterans of the previous year's festival, they got off to an incredibly bad start. The sound was appalling in both balance and quality, and the consequent lack of detail definition reduced their output to sheer boredom. They were also plagued by the anarchists, who diverted attention from the music by attempting to rip down the walls despite Farr's pronouncements. A seemingly interminable wait, while John Renbourne tuned his sitar and Bert Jansch did the same to his banjo, scarcely brought them favour either. But the lovely 'Light Flight' brought the audience back, and from there on in, they went from strength to strength, producing delightful versions of two old favourites, 'Bruton Town' and 'Pentangling'.

Bert Jansch – photographed backstage with Sandy Denny – explained the problems for acoustic musicians in these circumstances.

> *'You couldn't tell what you were sounding like. It's like asking a classical player to sit there while everybody's drinking. Some of the arrangements were so complex that if you screwed up, everybody screwed up.'*

Jacqui McShee had more pressing problems.

> *'The toilet facilities were dire. I always get nervous before performing, and all there was was just a latrine. A reporter told me that Joan Baez had her own loo, but wouldn't let anyone use it.'*

> *'A Pentacle, the word from which their name is derived, is a five-sided star. The Pentangle are five stars. They are also entertaining musicians.'*
> Programme note

It is also a word redolent of witchcraft, peculiarly appropriate in this setting. Afton Down itself is surmounted by neolithic burial mounds, and the chalk downs lead eastwards to a standing stone – where morris men dance at dawn on May morning – and *Five Barrows*, where it is not advisable to walk on certain dark nights.

MOODY BLUES

Mike Plumbley recalls, 'Their set was a stormer with the audience reacting to it by lighting up candles and matches and waving them as the night drew on.' The band travelled down from London by van, and stayed at a hotel in Sandown.

Whether roaring away on 'Ride My Seesaw' or taking it nice and easy on 'Sunset' from *Days Of Future Past* – with a flute solo from Ray Thomas and some atmospheric mellotron playing by Mike Pinder, the Moodies had long outgrown their early days as an R&B band from Birmingham, and indeed their performance at the previous year's festival. There was much praise for their vast sound system, loud yet well balanced, with all four voices coming through individually without distortion.

'Tuesday Afternoon' with its complex vocal harmonies and 'Never Comes The Day', with its switch of tempo in mid-stride, both benefited from this crystal clear sound, while the lyrics of 'Question' took on a new meaning, as they echoed around the open sky.

A (unintentionally) comic note was struck by drummer Graham Edge's recitation of his poem 'The Dream' in a flat, expressionless Brummie accent.

'Melancholy Man' began acoustically then in came a chorus and a plodding drum beat – one of the gloomiest and at the same time most exhilarating songs around. The band dedicated the song to compere Rikki Farr. 'Have You Heard' and the by now legendary 'Nights In White Satin' also stood out in a set which provoked warm applause.

One of the highlights of Murray Lerner's film, this majestic piece was sung by Justin Hayward with superb precision and feeling, and the soaring mellotron seemed to summon up darkness, as twilight faded from the downs. A spine tingling moment, even now.

JETHRO TULL

Their first appearance in England for nearly a year. Ian Anderson gave one of the finest individual performances of the entire five days, and

Jethro Tull emerged triumphant as one of the most entertaining and productive of all the bands. Ian appeared with beautiful long hair, especially washed for the occasion, a pair of natty long yellow combinations and a smart dressing gown with half the tails missing. Cocking his knee, grimacing, leaping, screaming, muttering, gibbering, sneezing, he looked like a brilliant but demented eighteenth-century German music master. He also knew exactly when to relinquish his gestures for the serious work of playing. His attitude to the mighty festival was also refreshing. 'It's like the Marquee, except bigger. Break down a fence and win a plastic bowl,' he muttered as they began to play 'My God'.

Anderson's acoustic guitar playing was something of a surprise, and one of the greatest musical assets of Tull proved to be keyboard player John Evan on 'With You There To Help Me', based on Beethoven's *Symphonie Pathetique*. Throughout John's piano solo, the flute player tried to upstage him. Comedy and the classics proved an interesting new form of mixed media.

When Ian wasn't amazing us with his flute playing, which leapt from the explosive to the beautiful, with Martin Barre's lead guitar and some brilliant drumming by Clive Bunker to enjoy.

They gained one of the biggest ovations of the Festival – they could have played all night if they had wanted. A tape in circulation comprises 'To Cry You A Song', 'Bouree', and 'Dharma For One', with a long and extremely boring drum solo. 'Nothing Is Easy' leads into 'We Used To Know', 'For A Thousand Mothers' and 'My Sunday Feeling', which appears in full technicolour in the *Message To Love* film. The set ends with 'My God' and 'With You To Help Me'.

Woodwind jazz-rock of the utmost excitement.

JIMI HENDRIX

Ralph McTell had earlier heard a roadie saying that Hendrix was 'very out of it' in someone's garden, and they were worried that he would not be up to playing. There was a nerve-racking delay of ninety minutes before his appearance. Part of this was taken up by DJ Jeff Dexter literally getting Hendrix together, using his portable sewing kit to pin up one of his sleeves, then repairing a split in the back of his trousers.

Pink Floyd's David Gilmour was pulled in from the crowd to help mix the sound.

It was the band's first appearance in England since Billy Cox joined as Noel Redding's replacement on bass. 'Yes, it has been a long time, hasn't it?' said a cool and impassive Jimi Hendrix, as he took the stage after the agonisingly long wait. He started with a distorted version of 'God Save The Queen' – which hardly anyone recognised – a counterpoint to his electronic demolition of the 'Star Spangled Banner' at Woodstock. Doubtless Commander Rees-Millington was suitably appalled – here was 'black power' in action – but why didn't someone tell Hendrix that it should have come at the end. That would certainly have cleared the crowd from the arena!

Hendrix was pencil thin and barely filled his multi-coloured smock – mainly in pink – apparently run up by a hallucinating tailor. With his newly trimmed afro hair-style, he looked tired and drawn, chewing gum throughout, but seemed determined to play, no matter what. Billy Cox proved solid if unimaginative on bass, but Mitch Mitchell was visually striking, like Animal in the Muppets, and a blur of energy behind the drum kit. Jimi's guitar playing seemed stiff and uninterested, which may have been due to the chill night air, or his mood that night. This uncertainty spread to the audience. At the end of one number there was no applause at all: some 600,000 souls sat in the darkness in total silence. Perhaps they had all fallen asleep. I know I almost did. The trio, no longer an Experience, were obviously under rehearsed and relying on magic and miracles, which seemed in short supply. Hendrix was like a tightrope walker plunging down to earth.

'All Along The Watchtower' came and went – Jimi muffed the words of the first verse – then as if to bring out the underlying tension, he dedicated the brutal, proto heavy metal 'Machine Gun' '...to all the skinheads fighting in Birmingham – uhy, and all the soldiers in Vietnam, I almost forgot, so many wars going on...'

The sound began to improve and Jimi's guitar picked up. 'They may be having an off-night, but he is still incredibly good,' said Peter Frampton, backstage. Around midnight Mitch played an inconclusive drum solo which didn't really help matters. It was as if he was playing only for himself. There was no reaction.

'Okay, we'll start all over again,' said Jimi. 'Hello, England.'

Suddenly, there was life on stage, and the band caught our attention as if for the first time. It was the sheer artistry and credibility of Hendrix's blues power that really began to turn the tide from disaster, especially 'Red House', always one of the highlights of his live performances. He now launched into a non-stop selection of known and unknown numbers – from the *First Ray Of The New Rising Sun* project – that got wilder and wilder.

Rod Allen describes the magic of Hendrix live, never quite captured on disc or film. You really had to be there.

'He plays the electronic and mechanical controls on his guitar as much as he plays the actual musical bits of it. He actually bends the notes – you can see them around you, curving.'

Security chief Victor Lewis remembers Hendrix staggering back to the amps and saying that he couldn't go on. Vic persuaded him to play just one more number, then carried the exhausted superstar – who collapsed as soon as he left the stage – over his shoulder and back to his caravan, like a multi-coloured sack of potatoes.

Hendrix's performance has steadily grown in critical esteem. It was perhaps his darkest concert, full of tension and the sense of something almost ended – the contrast with the first LP, bursting on its audience like a firework display of energy and new sounds is telling.

The *First Great Rock Festivals Of The Seventies* LP featured three songs, 'Power To Love', 'Midnight Lightning' and 'Foxy Lady'. In 1971, *Jimi Hendrix: Isle Of Wight* added 'Lover Man', 'Freedom', 'All Along The Watchtower' and 'In From The Storm', in a disappointing choice of material. Then in 1990, Murray Lerner premiered his Hendrix film, and the subsequent CD release featured almost an entirely different concert, in running order and tracks chosen. 'Intro'/'God Save The Queen', 'Message To Love', and 'Voodoo Chile' were all new, as were a twelve-minute 'Machine Gun', 'Dolly Dagger', an eleven-minute 'Red House' and 'New Rising Sun'. Only two tracks remained from the original release. To confuse matters further, the video soundtrack adds 'Message To Love', 'Sgt Pepper' and 'Spanish Castle Magic', and the concert was not in the order it happened but in a sequence which made most emotional sense.

The 'cat with the silver face' to whom Hendrix refers was apparently Nick Turner of Hawkwind, who was watching from the artists' enclosure near the front. Within three weeks, Hendrix was dead – on Friday 18 September, 1970 – just as his music seemed to be entering a new maturity and, it was being rumoured, that he would re-form the original Experience. He was as central to the development of rock music as a definitive art form as Louis Armstrong was to the history of jazz.

Martin Stone relates receiving a phone call from his friendly rival Peter Green:

'Martin, we're in trouble, I've got a tape of this new American guitarist who just played the Cromwellian, and he's so far ahead.'

As Stone told me, with Hendrix's arrival there were suddenly no limits as to what an electric guitar could achieve, and the places it could go. Perhaps in recognition of this, the ivory coloured Fender Strat Hendrix played at the IOW sold for auction in 1990 for £180,000.

Like Dylan and John Lennon, Hendrix remains central to the cultural identity of the late twentieth century.

In the *Melody Maker* published on 5 September, Hendrix talked about a future that history would deny him.

Q: Could Jimi give any indication when he would start to form the big band?
'I don't know, but it won't be very long. Isle of Wight might be the last, or the second to last. But if the kids really enjoyed it, then it might carry on a little longer. But I will only carry on that way if I am useful, you know you have to have a purpose in life.'

Q: His hair is a little tamer now. Did he feel he was a tamer person, a changing person?

161

'No I don't think so, although I feel as though I get little sparks of matureness every now and then. I think of tunes, I think of riffs. I can hum them. Then there's another melody comes into my head, and then a bass melody and then another one. On guitar I just can't get them out. I think I'm a better guitarist than I was. I've learned a lot. But I've got to learn more about music, because there's a lot in this hair (!) of mine that's got to get out.

'With the bigger band I don't want to be playing as much guitar. I want other musicians to play my stuff. I want to be a good writer. I still can't figure out what direction my writing is going at the moment, but I'll find a way.

'I won't be doing many live gigs, because I'm going to develop the sound and then put a film out with it. It's so exciting, it's going to be an audio/visual thing that you sit down and plug into, and really take in through your ears and eyes.

'I'm happy, it's gonna be good.'

A poignant moment occurred on Sunday night, when Jeff Dexter strolled to the mike and said, 'There's something I want to tell you.' Pregnant pause. 'Er, the stage is on fire.' This caused great merriment from the crowd. A firework, part of the evening's entertainment, had performed rather more enthusiastically than expected – another theory was that it was deliberate sabotage – and flames were spilling onto the roof. In the cold and desolation of two o'clock on Monday morning, it was eerily warming and comforting. There was no fear, no panic. 'Maybe it would all just go up in flames. And be done with.'

JOAN BAEZ

The finest folk singer in the world faced a hard job following the Hendrix noise, but her opening 'Let It Be' was meaningful under the circumstances, and her marvellous stage personality and springwater pure voice won the battle after just one number. After all that heavy, grinding rock and the mud and the grime and the crowded conditions and the airborne objects aimed at the stage like Exocet, Baez was a life-saver.

Standouts included a trio of Dylan songs – 'Farewell Angelina', 'I Shall Be Released' and 'Blowing In The Wind' – Leonard Cohen's 'Suzanne', 'Oh Happy Day', and 'The Night They Drove Old Dixie Down' from last year's joint headliners. She also charmed with Spanish songs and a haunting Italian ditty, as well as the traditional material with which she made her name, folk-songs like 'Silver Dagger'. Her confidence made everybody forget the cold, and demand encores – she was in complete command, and the audience took to her warmly.

By this time, Joan was more of a personality than a performer, but she certainly bridged the chasm between artist and audience, talking about her husband David, in prison for his opposition to Vietnam, and her new baby. Baez was best when singing unaccompanied, half a million people quietly listening to her *a cappella* version of the gospel song 'Swing Low Sweet Chariot', as if they were all seated around the same camp fire. And she was surprisingly funny.

> *'No, I'm not getting £30,000, or whatever, for this one and I'm not living on some luxury yacht. Leonard Cohen and I are staying in a nice little hotel around here, with breakfast at a quarter to nine.'*

Not being Joni Mitchell, this last remark raised no *Carry On* innuendo. Rod Allen:

> *'It was an interesting idea to put Hendrix on before Joan Baez. The nice thing is that it worked, completely. Hendrix did his thing and stimulated one set of glands, and Joan Baez did hers and stimulated an entirely different set of glands. Isn't that nice.'*

LEONARD COHEN AND THE ARMY

After all the excitement and weariness, Cohen provided the perfect antidote, as relaxing and nourishing as a cup of Horlicks. His backing band was quite magical – not least backing vocalists Aileen Fowler and Corlynn Hanney – not least on 'Lady Midnight', one of his most melodic, caressing songs. Ron Cornelius played guitar, Charlie Daniels bass and violin, and Bob Johnston – Dylan's record producer – guested on harmonica. In a ritual which had not then been cheapened with over use, Cohen requested that everyone light a match. Thousands of tiny flames lit Afton Down like a giant Christmas tree.

The Canadian poet played a gentle, relaxed, musicianly set in the early morning rain which those not already waiting in line for the Southern Vectis buses received with acclaim. He had been a little nervous before. 'There are so many people on, and so many that I want to see. I'm not a top rank star you see, no I'm not a top-ranker,' he told *Melody Maker* later.

Cohen stood behind a pillar, praying, before he went on stage. Perhaps this was to deflect hostile criticism from the music press, but if so it did not succeed.

> *'After that performance they wrote about me, "Leonard Cohen is a boring old drone and should go the fuck back to Canada where he belongs."'*

Cohen's critical reputation has since been restored. 'Tonight Will Be Fine' appears back on the IOW Festival compilation LP and on *Live Songs*, released in 1973. One of the highlights of *Message To Love* is Cohen's version of 'Suzanne', with celestial backing.

RICHIE HAVENS

It fell to Richie Havens – who had opened Woodstock and preceded Dylan and the Band at Wootton – to make the final exit of the final festival.

Havens, with his long time guitarist Paul Williams playing as brilliantly as ever, went through a mostly familiar set in which he successfully recreated the excitement of his Woodstock rendition of 'Sometimes I Feel Like a Motherless Child'/'Freedom', and he ended on a high note with the Hare Krishna mantra.

He performed 'Here Comes The Sun' just as the sun rose. His gutsy singing softened the dawn. Charles Everest – whenever about to photograph him – recalls that Havens would turn his head to show off his impressive profile. He sang 'Freedom' with a poignant power that raised the spirits of the small huddled circles of those music fans who remained. I remember that it all seemed like a wake, sad but beautiful, with this man pouring out his heart and soul. We brought him back with thunderous applause after the Hare Krishna mantra to do 'Run, Shaker, Life' and with that he sent us home.

So that was the 1970 IOW Festival. Someone, maybe Rikki Farr, announced, 'You've all been beautiful! Even those who tore down the fences.'

'When I sing my mind is busy looking at the pictures the writer created. My body has something to do, which is play the guitar. And my spirit is feeling the song's sensations all over again. It's like this. I sing from what I see. It goes out and then it comes back to me.'
Programme note

The Fiery Creations' chauffeur recalls driving with Havens to a small hotel in Shanklin at seven o'clock that morning. 'He rather startled the landlady. He took his teeth out and said, "Hello". He put it all on!'

There was a sense of things ending, of a dream dissolving the morning rain. In *Days In The Life*, Charles Shaar Murray described the feeling. 'That was when my first wave of disillusionment with hippies set in.' He went up to Richard Neville, upset and stoned, and said, 'You realise this thing's over.' Murray had bought the idea that life could be an endless free rock festival, and reality had suddenly caught up.

It was like the end of a holiday. Now it was time to get back to work. Mrs Thatcher was waiting in the wings, and would be in power by the end of the decade. A generation brought up to expect an all-encompassing welfare state to look after them from cradle to grave, would have to learn the hard way that nothing was free in this life. Hopefully, the music that all three festivals had broadcast would provide a touchstone of joy and fellow feeling with which to live one's life. In the bleak times ahead – with 'no such thing as society' – it would be something to hang on to.

Monday saw a Dunkirk style evacuation of the Island, as the site turned into...

> '...*the longest bus queue we had ever seen: two queues wound for about a mile from camp sites on opposite sides of the arena, but the wet and windswept fans shifted slowly forward in surprisingly patient and orderly fashion.*'

As *Zigzag* reported, even the previous day, when the gates were finally thrown open it was only to reveal a three-hour queue of people waiting to go home.

The Foulks too had disappeared from the site, to barricade themselves in Inglefield, keeping a mass of creditors at bay. On stage, things had been abandoned to Jeff Dexter. The Revd Bowyer was attempting to organise a scheme for kids with no money to help clear the arena in return for their fares home, but he had met catcalls and boos from some of the crowd, who discerned (wrongly) a Fiery Creations rip-off. This provoked the final Rikki Farr freak out, a tirade, which ended, 'To all the good kids who came here I say goodbye. To the rest of you, go to hell.'

Rolling Stone provided a stark picture of life behind the scenes.

> '*Midnight Sunday, Ray Foulk paced through the loose dirt behind the stage, his eyes empty, his mouth trembling. His Brylcreemed hair was starting to coagulate into lumps, his thin tie to unknot. "I've lost," he snarled with quaking voice, "faith in everything".*'

As morning arrived, and the music ended, the weather changed with symbolic abruptness. The sun which had beaten down uninterrupted for three days vanished, replaced by a biting wind and a cold intermittent drizzle. What had begun as a pilgrimage, ended with shivers and sneezes, though the returning fans seemed to retain their good humour. One lady left with the comment, 'I think the movie will be better!' As one friend remembers:

'I walked down into Freshwater, munching some windfall apples. The residents were all friendly – it took all day to get the bus back to Ryde; people didn't care about the rain or the queues. A man in a little grocery store said that it was the best time ever on the Island. Everyone was nice to each other. One girl danced topless, amid a general consensus that she should cover up. The stalls were mainly junk food and tie-die shops and record stalls. Jeff Dexter played the Airplane's 'We Can Be Together' and Fairport's 'Jigs And Reels', which resulted in a massive square dance. The toilets were grim, though!'

And so the third and greatest Isle of Wight Festival came to its gentle, weary conclusion. It had been taking part in a great battle – confusing, epic, full of sudden shafts of tragedy and light relief. As the generals flew off in helicopters to their luxury hotels – and, in the case of the Foulks, it was rumoured a cruise on the *QEII* – the foot soldiers returned to their humble tents, and appalling latrines.

My own abiding memory as I set off for home and a warm bath was of watching one poor unfortunate fall into the slit trench which served as a mass open-air commode. That and a great feeling of excitement, exhaustion and fellow feeling. Society was more of a garden, less of a jungle, in those far-off days.

May they return soon.

The Afton event was the last of its kind. Only Live Aid ever fully recaptured the atmosphere and spirit of the final IOW event, because those who participated were looking outside themselves, suspending disbelief that as ordinary people they were powerless. Rock music itself has since become a consumer commodity, carefully delineated into mutually warring factions. The sense of tribal purpose and sheer optimism has long gone, though perhaps it is now returning.

In one of the most honest accounts of the Afton event, T.P. Kelsey stated the view from the arena, a personal summation of what those five days of music meant to those who experienced them, a blueprint for a more hopeful future.

'And when it was all over and the long files of fans were waiting for their transport back home, I felt most of them must have been proud to have been part of the third Isle of Wight Festival of Music. For the festival provided an alternative society. A society where people forgot their own particular class, creed, race or religion and were able to live together and do the simple things of life on a friendly basis. There's something in that, I'm sure. Think about it.'

14

The aftermath

Back to the clerk of Freshwater Parish Council, monitoring the seismic shocks of this earthquake. A week after the Festival, he records 'many complaints regarding litter from the site blowing under high winds onto the main highway causing danger to drivers; large sheets of polythene plastic a particular hazard'. The following are particularly hysterical, but not untypical:

> 'This was no pop festival, it was an excuse for a glorified orgy and it paid off. I feel sick to think people will have to eat the wheat from the fields where these filthy louts did their business.'

> 'Such a thing is of Satan whose every moral principle is let loose.'

> 'At Freshwater Bay there was more nudity, sexual gropings and cleaners were finding contraceptive pills and drug pills lying on beach and promenade. Hedgerows became urinals, and crop fields were used as toilets by both sexes who squatted

*in the cereals to relieve themselves. Many of these people had
head lice clearly visible.'*

The journalist Anthony Haden-Guest writing in the *Daily Telegraph* –
hardly a bastion of hippie values – came up with a more judicious
overview.

*'Togetherness. Joan Baez claims it, Joni Mitchell pleads for it,
and Tiny Tim adulates it. Pete Townshend pokes fun at it, the
Voices Of East Harlem demonstrate it, and Richie Havens,
closing the show, says that is what he is all about. Only Miles
Davis seems to ignore it, doing what he does best, then gliding
off stage, avoiding communion with the crowd.'*

Haden-Guest puts the pop festival in context as an 'orgasmic upsurge
of the sixties', like the moon landings or the mini-skirt. He discerns
that two contradictory myths about them peddled by the media, that
of outrage – sex and drugs in the grass – and that of Utopia, a state of
secular grace. Even in the 'bitter blueness of early morning Monday',
with pirate vendors selling hot dogs for four shillings and asking ten
shillings for twenty cigarettes, there are signs of hope, of attempts to
bring the second of these two myths into reality.

*'Communal kitchens develop in the obliterated snack bars,
and on my final morning I queue up for free breakfast of soup
and grey home-made bread smeared with – of all things – a
donated tin of pate de foie. Release and half a dozen other
voluntary organisations are taking care of upwards of a
thousand kids stranded without money, identities, passports,
destinations.'*

Here one sees a move towards compassion, towards a more
wholesome diet, and in general a better ecological balance between
consumption and production. It is like the conclusion of Andrew
Sinclair's bizarre novel *Magog*, where the hero – a captain of industry
– reaches some kind of death vision at the Afton site, and is reborn as
a more socially concerned person. 'He stooped and picked a bit of
litter from the grass. Beginning to put the world right.'

In his book *Isle Of Wight 1970: The Last Great Festival*, Rod Allen takes up this point. Despite the hippie jargon, his words prove strangely prophetic:

> *'Fire, earth, air and water. It's a pity we don't take more care of the elements we celebrate... why do people let caterers sell coke in aluminium cans at festivals, for instance. You can't recycle them, you can't burn them, and they consume enormous quantities of electricity to produce. We ought to think more, we ought to care more. Perhaps we will.'*

It is no accident that in Murray Lerner's movie, one of the most articulate and determined of the 'Desolation Row' protesters should grow up to become perhaps the leading Island conservationist. From 'tear down the walls' to 'preserve the walls'! Rod Allen also predicts correctly the way forward in financing these huge events, although he gets the reason wrong. Commercial pragmatism, not idealism, was to fuel the move towards corporate sponsorship.

> *'What we were witnessing was the end of the rip-off form in festivals. Tomorrow's festivals – like the 1970 Rotterdam Festival – will be free to the people, and the bills will be paid by giant advertisers as part of their new social-conscience kick... putting money back into the community they have taken so much out of. Coca-Cola paid for Rotterdam; British Rail should have paid for the IOW – everyone had to use the BR ferry at ten bob a round trip.'*

The ferries were privatised in the 1980s. The army of denimed freaks at the IOW largely became the new middle class professionals: media workers, market researchers, management theorists, corporate executives, social workers, teachers in further education.

One thing that Allen got seriously wrong was the attitude to money: 'The hill people had it right – they made it free.' A harder, meaner, more cynical, more pressurised world was waiting just around the corner, one where money was a goal rather than a tool. Fools gold indeed for all but the lucky few, as recession bit deep in the late 1980s.

When one thinks back over twenty-five years which have brought us the Falklands War, the Gulf War, Rwanda, Bosnia and innumerable other conflicts, it is ironic to read that 'at that point we really all learned the meaning of the peace sign – a symbol of our people in America. Two fingers held proudly in the air is now a sign of brotherhood and love.'

This is particularly ironic when one considers some of the footage captured by Murray Lerner, which resemble downtown Beirut or some of the industrial conflicts of the early eighties. It must be said that *Message To Love* conflates various incidents, some of which took place before the Festival proper had even begun. On the other hand, what Lerner captures, even out of context, is a symbolic moment of liberation. The tearing down of this rusting ironwork prefigures the destruction of the Berlin wall.

In 1970, who would have dared predict the peaceful end of the Soviet empire. Perhaps Afton was a kind of precursor to the EEC. 'Also important is the huge number of Europeans who came over. Announcements were made from the stage in French, German and Italian, and I personally was surrounded by foreign people all the time I was there.' So was I, and if I remember one of them kept kicking me in the back for two solid days.

Allen concludes that: 'Festivals are all about kicking out the jams. You're stardust; what festivals can do for you is get you back into the garden.' In this he was certainly right. If nothing else, most of the denizens of the IOW Festival I know are regular visitors to their local garden centre!

Wine writer Hugh Johnson summed things up for the *Daily Telegraph*.

'I enjoyed it all right, in the same uncritical way I enjoyed The Ten Commandments or The Robe and for the grand simple values in landscape – a final uprearing of chalk before the sea. The orange and blue and green of the tents swelled in the hollows and crowned the ridge, marching away over fields smeared with the smoke of campfires.

'To enjoy it was easy, to define it harder. Comparisons suggested themselves: medieval fairs, the country souks of Morocco, Derby Day, but there were also moments when I

thought I was stepping among the flake-outs from a great youth
hostel trek. The pennants saying Windemere and Snowdon
peeped out from under the fringes and the beards.
  'The only violence was provoked by the hideous corrugated
iron walls around the show. You missed nothing but the
pressure of bodies by staying outside, climbing the hill, and
enjoying a heavenly view through the misty sunlight over the
fields and woods to the tilting white sails in the Solent.'

'Now, just wait for the film,' Rikki says happily, standing on the stage, deserted now, apart from a vandalised grand piano. 'It's going to be bigger than Woodstock. Much bigger,' says Farr. 'And you know what we want to call it. *The Last Great Event.*'

Message To Love – as it was retitled, after the Hendrix song – finally emerged for public viewing twenty-five years later, in autumn 1995. A requiem for the sixties, it has been edited for maximum impact, so that the film opens with the white cliffs of England, and in bright sunshine. Things darken, into a near riot, and the film ends in rain, with young hippies beginning the long trek home, in slow motion. Both film and Festival take on the shape of a human life, from birth through the getting of wisdom, through experience, to funeral rites.

As we have seen, this inverts the chronology of the fence busting, which mostly took place before the Festival had really begun, and takes some of Rikki Farr's outbursts out of context, but it does make dramatic and symbolic sense. The use of music to counterpoint the action is masterful throughout. For instance, Tiny Tim's pious twitterings about music being free is undercut by Bert Block's cynical realism – he wouldn't even tune his ukulele until paid in pound notes – and we are straight into Taste performing 'Sinner Boy'.

Again, Ray Foulk's spat with the manager of Chicago, obsessed with his band's place at the top of the pecking order, is followed by the Doors' 'When The Music's Over'. The quality of the performances – in both musical and recording terms – is startling, and rewrites history in terms of both Hendrix and the Doors, who give everything, admittedly to bleak visions and threatening chords, as if mourning something departing their world. Like hope.

The Foulk brothers and Rikki Farr also shed their public image of the time – fostered by the likes of Mick Farren – as rip-off businessmen, and come over as tough but idealistic youths, determined to take on the large corporations and 'mohair suits' in a kind of prefiguring of Mrs Thatcher's 'popular capitalism'. If the corporate world is back in charge these days, it is hardly their fault. They come over as witty and committed – while foxily canny – whereas their opponents on the barricades come over as self-righteous, morally confused and out of control. Looking back, Mick Farren is a far more threatening and dangerous character than, say Rikki Farr. It was Farren who had himself photographed at the time marching down a London street leading his acolytes, all dressed impeccably in Nazi uniform.

The film also introduces us to some unforgettable characters behind the scenes. Bud the stoned carpenter – a Woodstock veteran from Mill Valley, California. Bert Block delivering witty, cynical lines to camera like Bob Hope. The Dutch Baroness Patsy Boudensijan, a girlfriend of yachtsman Uffa Fox, and famed throughout the whole of the Island for the size of her... personality. Commander William Rees-Millington RN with his jabbing pipe and his conspiracy theories.

Reviewing the film in the *Daily Mail*, Philip Norman noted how:

> '...*the film presents a mesmerising cavalcade of talent soon to meet the destiny of those who live too hard and too fast: Jimi Hendrix, gaudy in luminous pink with his erotic guitar and strangely gentle voice, Jim Morrison on his way to his weird destiny as a shrine in Paris and the Who's steroid-eyed, grimacing "Moon the Loon". Here too is a crowd in whom Love and Peace are already noticeably on the wane.*'

No wonder Rikki Farr ends the film saying how he suddenly feels himself to be an older, sadder man. The rain from which he shelters could be the tears of a lost generation.

15

The final analysis?

I n 1971, Roy Carr of the *New Musical Express* interviewed Rikki Farr about the past, the present, and the future.

Q: Do you think that the days of the big rock festivals are over?
'Yes, they are over.'

Q: What in your opinion has killed it?
'The whole system of how they are put on. I personally hate security men and guard dogs... it's against all the basic principles of a festival. But you have to go through all the ludicrous expense of having to do it because of a minority whose only objective in coming to a festival is gross vandalism.'

Q: Though musically successful, both the Woodstock and the IOW festivals suffered a great financial loss and a breakdown in organisation. From your experience, do you think it is still possible to promote a successful event on such a gargantuan scale?

'Yes, we feel that the Foulk brothers and myself have enough knowledge to do the thing properly. Not only that, we also have tremendous sources of information at our disposal and I feel that we have learned from our mistakes. There can be no better substitute than the sheer experience of actually staging such an event.'

Q: So what went wrong at the IOW?
'Ignorance and misunderstanding. If you work it out, at the IOW each artist cost two bob a head to see, plus the two free days that we gave at our own expense.'

Q: There are reports that some of the artists who appeared didn't get paid. Is that correct?
'They were part-paid; they didn't get their full fee for the simple reason that there wasn't any money to pay them. The artists in question were the Moody Blues, Taste, Leonard Cohen and ELP. Once the situation was fully explained to them, their reaction was marvellous. Joan Baez offered to do a benefit concert for us in London. I didn't accept the offer because she had already given her fee to an orphanage, and we felt that she had done more than her bit.'

Q: What was the budget you set for the IOW Festival?
'£280,000.'

Q: How much did you lose?
'£125,000.'

Q: But didn't you sell enough tickets in advance to cover the cost?
'No. But if everybody who came to the Festival had paid then we would have made a profit. As it was, the White Panthers distributed leaflets to tell people not to pay as the walls were going to be breached, and like Woodstock it would be made a free festival. Also we were forced by the Council onto a site which we knew and they knew was totally unsuitable both sound-wise and security-wise. We gave out 10,000 free tickets

to the people on the hill and to those who claimed that they didn't have the money to get in. They sold those tickets and still broke the walls down and then said it was all a big rip-off.'

Q: Would you say that trouble at festivals is organised?
'Yes. As a promoter you are always naked to the subversive deviant who comes from behind you wailing his propaganda. I can only hope that their intelligence will in future allow them to think a little more clearly about what and why they are attacking.'

Q: Do you think perhaps people are frightened of you because you are so outspoken in your views?
'Politicians call me a communist... they think I am trying to undermine the youth culture. The underground call me a capitalist... I'm neither. I've been accused of being a hired gun, a God-freak, a junkie, a fascist, an anarchist, a communist, a conservative, a con-man, a liar and a thief. If they kill me, Ronan O'Rahily and people like us, then this business is going to be a very quiet place.'

Q: Do you feel a responsibility towards the safety of the people who attend your festivals?
'Totally, the reason I compere the shows, sometimes very badly, is because I feel that at such large gatherings of people, especially those sitting far away from the stage, they must feel that there is a vulnerable human being trying to build a bridge from the stage to them. There was a moment at the IOW when I asked the audience to hold hands, the emotion of which I could never explain. Never in the history of the world has that amount of people joined hands together in a field without being under the standard of a military flag. On that account alone, I feel the Festival was an unqualified success.'

Q: Does this mean that you intend to stage another festival?
'Yes, most definitely. It's like gardening, your fingers get green

and you can't stop. I hope to do something on a smaller scale next year, but next year following the IOW film we plan a real bonanza.'

Disc for 6 March, 1971 announced: *'There my yet be another IOW Festival!'*. Ray Foulk announced that he had arranged full American distribution for a three-hour film on the 1970 event, even now being given a final cut on the Island. And that was the last thing officially heard about the film until late summer 1995.

Later that month, *Disc* carried an update on the Festival story. It would be a three-day event for around 100,000 people and was being planned to beat the forthcoming Parliamentary bill to restrict events to twenty-four hours maximum. Three sites were actively under consideration, none of which was Afton Down; it would be a gentler occasion, with more folk music 'instead of the heavy lot we've had over the last two years'.

This story of a planned sequel to the three Island pop festivals – IOW IV – has run for twenty-four years, and a separate book could be written about all the rumours, the botched attempts, the broken promises, the good ideas broken on the wheel of local bureaucracy and Masonic handshakes. It is as if the 'mohair suits' about whom the Foulks joked had waited for their revenge, and were determined that such fun should never be had again. As I know to my own cost!

The 1971 event was planned despite the liquidation of Fiery Creations. Minutes are still in existence of a music sub-committee of the County Council, a majority of the members of which were well known opponents of the previous events. Hardly a level playing field. Three meetings in May were concerned with finding good reasons against all six submitted sites. A meeting held on 6 August was more upbeat, perhaps because Ray Foulk had already made a press statement that no festival would now take place. The County Council had obtained an injunction in the High Court, delaying things until the implementation of the Isle of Wight County Council Act 1971.

Introduced in the 1970-71 session of Parliament, and still in force, this prohibited an overnight gathering of more than 5,000 people in the open air. There was surprisingly little resistance from civil libertarians on this outrageous abuse of freedom, like a panic measure brought in during war time, rather than a considered response. It is the spiritual heir to the recent Criminal Justice Act, and likewise subverts that side of the English spirit which believes in free expression and individual rights.

It was left to the maverick Tom Driberg to act as the official opposition. He read out a description by John Wesley of the tremendous impact of the great open air gatherings he addressed as part of his evangelical revival. *Hansard* recorded the fall out.

Mr Ogden: My hon Friend is surely not suggesting that a pop festival on the Isle of Wight has any relationship in spirit with those gatherings. I happen to be a Methodist. The two might be the same in numbers but not in spirit.

Mr Driberg: I believe that pop is a kind of religion of the young. It may be a kind of Dionysian religion in some instances.

Sir Charles Taylor: Fornication.

Mr Driberg: It fills them with a kind of exaltation, a euphoria. It has nothing to do with drugs or sex. It is the getting together of thousands of young people to enjoy and share an experience which exalts them.

Mr Frank Judd: Some churchmen who were present at the Festival have all borne witness to the fact that there were elements of spirituality present in that gathering which they as Christians found extremely impressive.

Sir C. Taylor: Fornication.

Mr Driberg: I wish the Member for Eastbourne would not keep interjecting 'Fornication' from a sedentary position. He seems obsessed with the subject.

Rear-Admiral Morgan-Giles: Even the hon Gentleman must surely realise that if he is recommending a substitution of pop festivals for any type of religious observance he will cause a great deal of offence on both sides of the House.

At this point, Driberg read out a letter from *The Times* which declared that: *'For five days all barriers of class, creed and nationality were totally ignored. People shared their food, money and possessions with complete strangers, and the "natural reserve" of the British were entirely forgotten.'*

Tom Driberg: These young people were behaving like the earliest Christians in the Acts of the Apostles, who had all things in common.

Mr Patrick Cormack: What nauseating claptrap.

For all this, the bill was carried by 107 votes to six. The long-term effects of this and other attempts to legally control and curtail large open air events were later analysed by Michael Clarke in *The Politics Of Pop Festivals*.

> '*Commercial promoters, having lost money and seen others do so, became much more cautious, and in their place the free festival began to come to prominence, run by amateurs.*'

Meanwhile, the Foulks were elsewhere, covering another green-field site with hippies. In September 1971, they brought rock music to the Oval cricket ground, its pitch covered with giant mats for the occasion. A one-day charity concert for famine relief in Bangladesh drew 10,000, many of whom had queued all night: the Surrey Tavern stayed open all night supplying soup to the masses. Inside, the Who headlined. Outside, a hundred security men patrolled solid twelve foot brick perimeter walls. Other veterans of the Isle of Wight to appear were Cochise, whose lead guitarist had appeared with Plastic Penny in 1968, and the Grease Band without Joe Cocker.

A weariness seemed to be descending. In *The Road Goes On Forever*, Philip Norman captures this in his essay on the Foulks and two further Oval concerts they promoted the following year, one featuring Frank Zappa and Hawkwind – who had played free in 1970 outside the main site – the other headlining Emerson, Lake And Palmer. There is a hungover, Monday morning atmosphere, a sense as Peter Bull puts it that 'we're not feeling anything come back any more'. As Norman himself points out, 'The festivity has gone out of Rock, in any venue.'

It would take the incendiary fire of the Sex Pistols to bring back danger and celebration into rock music, even if they seemed to spit on everything that the IOW festivals stood for. Musically, bands like Teardrop Explodes, the Stone Roses and Oasis would later tap into the mix of controlled aggression and some kind of spiritual awareness, exuded by the best sixties bands. Meanwhile, the likes of Blur were resurrecting the kind of quality pop which the IOW festivals had been largely instrumental in rubbing out in the first place!

The big difference, following on from the Thatcher years, was the rise of acid house and rave, large open air, night-time parties lit by a newly discovered drug, Ecstasy, which brought on just those feelings of loving one's fellow humans and the need for a community which the great festivals had fostered, yet failed to sustain.

There was a dance element to this new music missing since audiences had began to sit down and treat rock concerts like some kind of art performance. This change was particularly noticeable at the Glastonbury festivals, which themselves were a continuation of the best aspects of the 1970 Festival, but smaller in scale, wider in scope.

On the Island, the annual Garlic Fair – with its sense of a community at peace with itself – does much the same. In 1990, I was involved with a revival event, held at a Ryde sports stadium. Musicians from the original festivals – the Third Ear Band, Julie Felix, the Groundhogs – seemed less in tune with that spirit than the post-punk performers. Captain Sensible's guitar blazed like Hendrix's – and he exposed himself like Jim Morrison – while Boy George sang mantras, backed by saffron robed monks. Only Dick Taylor seemed timeless, still ready as a musician to experiment and learn.

What I personally found most depressing was the backstage antics of some of the performers; it seemed the less talent they had ever possessed, the more ready they were to demand instant payment and superstar treatment. One famous rock lyricist threatened to send round some 'boys from the smoke' to my home if he wasn't paid in full there and then. He wasn't; my legs remain intact. I spent the next morning hiding in the leisure centre toilet as local radio reporters and angry creditors circled the building. Suddenly, I felt a strong surge of sympathy for Ray Foulk.

He too re-emerged. In autumn 1993, a press conference was held at Farringford, Tennyson's old home, to announce a five-year programme by the Leading Edge Foundation to promote the world's premier musical event on the Island, featuring everything from Pavarotti to a permanent pop festival site. Foulk's enemies were better organised and funded this time. Two years on, the idea is still on the drawing board, and a planned 1995 event with the return of Bob Dylan and virtually every leading rock band of our times was scuppered by the

Council's refusal to grant a licence. One of the reasons given was the somewhat odd excuse that such a festival would be bad for tourism – this for a man who had brought more paying customers to the Island than even Fred Pontin.

Undeterred, Foulk is planning a multi-stage event for next summer to take place on the island or close to it, mixing rock with classical music and opera. This prompts Philip Norman to a vision which restores Wight to its ancient place as 'The White Island', a place of spiritual refreshment and earth mysteries.

'So the shades of Tennyson, Keats and Macaulay may be aroused all over again. And maybe those of Hendrix, Jim Morrison, Keith Moon and Miles Davis along with them. Now that's what I call a supergroup.'

Such a concert is perhaps beyond the powers even of Ray Foulk. What the Island got instead on August Bank Holiday Saturday was a small event organised by the local radio station as part of their appeal to raise funds for a scanner for Newport hospital. Sharing the bill with the Love Affair and P.J. And Duncan were the Pretty Things, virtually reformed to their 1968 line-up, and Ray Dorset, of Mungo Jerry. At long last he had made it onto an Island stage, twenty-five years too late.

16

Requiem for the past

Early evening, Saturday 26 August, 1995. A strange event takes place that will live long in the memory of the hundred or so people who attend, and which acts as a kind of requiem for the 1970 IOW Festival.

Rock eccentric Robyn Hitchcock, whose band the Soft Boys had purveyed a weird mix of punk and psychedelia in the late seventies, gives an acoustic concert at Yarmouth railway station – one of a series of free events for members of his fan club. The fact that trains have not called at Yarmouth station, now a youth centre, for over thirty years merely adds to the dream-like quality of the event. Hitchcock stands where the tracks had once been, to an audience draped around the platform.

He dedicates his set to the memory of Jimi Hendrix, who had performed just across the hill twenty-five years before. He begins with 'Are You Experienced', and later performs 'The Wind Cries Mary'. Hitchcock talks of what Hendrix's set had meant to him, and how bizarre it was to pass through Freshwater nowadays. The public loo which he had queued at with a crocodile of hippies in loon pants and long hair is still there, but always ominously empty. He talks about an army of people who had arrived and left, as if they had never been, then sings some of his own twisted narratives of ghosts and crustaceans, and dreaming of trains.

He blows some Dylan-like harmonica, and reminisces on the '69 Festival, and making a pilgrimage to see a white dot trying to sing like Johnny Cash, then performed spooky versions of 'It Takes A Lot To Laugh, It Takes A Train To Cry' and – holy writ – 'Visions Of Johanna', in which he changes one line to *jellyfish women*', and thus makes the song his own. He even talks about his own free concert, and asks us all to give a donation to ourselves when we get home!

Hitchcock's most personal song of the evening, 'Element Of Light' is set at Compton Bay – where naked hippies had once danced in a ritual circle – and which is now rapidly eroding. People walking its cliffs would return one day as ghosts far out to sea, out of their natural element.

Hendrix too had stepped out of time. He would now remain forever the age that he died; unlike us he would never grow old. On which thought, we disperse to the pub, glad to be alive, aware that with time all memories will be swept away, even that of Hendrix, even that of the greatest rock festival that ever was.

And then most of us go back home, to watch the first public showing of Murray Lerner's film of The Last Great Event, to recreate the time of our lives...

Appendices

Select bibliography

This account of the Island festivals draws on a large body of printed and visual information. The material listed here is an extremely small part of the whole. I have concentrated on what is most easily accessible, and relevant.

1968
Geoff Wall: 'It Was Twenty Years Ago Today...', *Holding Together* 7 (1988) pp 18–19.

1969
1969 *Festival Programme*, 48 pp.
Charles Laurence: 'Ticket To Ryde', *Telegraph Weekend Magazine*, 16 August 1989, pp 10–17.
Fourth Time Around 3 – Special Dylan on the IOW issue, 36 pp.

1970
Festival Fun Book, *London Evening Standard*, 22 August 1970, 24 pp.
1970 *Festival Programme*, 48 pp.
Rod Allen: *Isle Of Wight 1970: The Last Great Festival*, Clipper Press

(1970) 60 pp.

Anthony Haden-Guest, 'The Last Great Event', *Daily Telegraph Magazine*, 30 December 1970, pp 18–26.

Andrew Sinclair: *Magog*, Weidenfeld & Nicholson (1972). A novel whose final scenes take place at the Afton Festival.

'Eyewitness Special: The 1970 Isle Of Wight Festival', *Q* Magazine 108, September 1995, pp 56–64.

Trevor Dann: 'When Love Broke Down', *Times Magazine*, 19 August 1995, pp 24–29.

General

Michael Clarke: *The Politics Of Pop Festivals*, Junction Books (1982).

Philip Norman: *The Road Goes On Forever*, Elm Tree (1972), 'The Foulk Brothers; Pop Promoting Blues', pp 258–269.

Jonathon Green: *Days In The Life, Voices From The English Underground*, Heinemann (1988).

'The Great Sixties Festivals: Isle of Wight', *Record Collector* 120 (August 1989), pp 39–41.

Brian Hinton: *Nights In Wight Satin*, IOW Cultural Services (1990).

Richard Neville: *Hippie Hippie Shake*, Bloomsbury (1995).

Vic King, Mike Plumbley & Pete Turner: *Isle Of Wight Rock*, Rock Archives (1995).

Film and video

Jimi Hendrix

Warner Home Video (1988)

Originally a film made for the cinema, assembled by Joe Boyd – Fairport's manager in 1968. Three songs from the 1970 Festival appearance were used: 'Machine Gun', 'In From The Storm' and 'Red House'.

Jimi Hendrix At The Isle Of Wight

BMG Video (1990)

This was premiered at the National Film Institute in September 1990, twenty years after Hendrix's death, and was introduced by Murray Lerner. He explained that this fifty-seven minute video was a taster for the ultimate IOW 1970 film, which actually emerged five years later. It saw limited cinema release, some screenings introduced by Vivian Stanshall, which must have been a real experience. Eleven songs, digitally mastered: 'Message To Love', 'God Save The Queen', 'Sgt Pepper', 'Spanish Castle Magic', 'All Along The Watchtower', 'Voodoo Chile', 'Freedom', 'Machine Gun', 'Dolly Dagger', 'Red House' and 'In From The Storm'.

Free
Island (1989)
Three songs were filmed on the IOW in 1970: 'Mr Big', 'Be My Friend' and 'All Right Now'. There are also fine aerial shots of the Festival site.

Message To Love
Castle Communications (1995)
First broadcast on BBC 2 on Saturday 26 August, 1995 to mark the twenty-fifth anniversary of the 1970 Festival. Buried treasure, and (almost) the full story! The video features live performances and *cinéma-vérité* film of the 1970 Festival, including music by the Who, Ten Years After, Joni Mitchell, Joan Baez, Kris Kristofferson, the Doors, Miles Davis, Jimi Hendrix, Donovan, Taste, Tiny Tim, Jethro Tull, Moody Blues, Free, Emerson Lake And Palmer, Leonard Cohen and John Sebastian.

Discography

LPs and CDs

LEONARD COHEN
Live Songs
CBS (1973)
'Tonight Will Be Fine' is taken from his IOW appearance in 1970.

BOB DYLAN
Self Portrait
CBS (1970)
'Like A Rolling Stone', 'Quinn The Eskimo', 'Minstrel Boy' and 'She Belongs To Me', all backed by the Band, come from the second Isle of Wight Festival. And to think that CBS released this material in preference to the 1966 tour with very much the same band.

JIMI HENDRIX
Jimi Hendrix: Isle Of Wight
Polydor (1971)
Side one: 'Midnight Lightning', 'Foxy Lady', 'Lover Man'.

Side two: 'Freedom', 'All Along The Watchtower', 'In From The Storm'. All tracks are from 1970.

Jimi Hendrix: Isle Of Wight
Polydor (1988)
CD reissue of the above.

Live Isle Of Wight '70
Polydor (1991)
'Intro'/'God Save The Queen', 'Message To Love', 'Voodoo Chile', 'Lover Man', 'Machine Gun', 'Dolly Dagger', 'Red House', 'In From The Storm', 'New Rising Sun'.
CD which advertises seven previously unreleased tracks. Packaging contains colour shots from the Murray Lerner film.

TASTE
Taste Live At The Isle Of Wight
Polydor (1971)
Side one: 'What's Going On', 'Sugar Mama', 'Morning Sun', 'Sinner Boy'
Side two: 'Feel So Good', 'Catfish'.
All tracks taken from the 1970 Festival. The front cover shows Taste on stage, the back cover is a fine colour photograph of the Festival audience, with Afton Down in the background.

VARIOUS
The First Great Rock Festivals Of The Seventies: Isle Of Wight, Atlanta Pop Festival
CBS (1971)
Sly and the Family Stone: 'Stand', 'You Can Make It If You Try'
Cactus: 'No Need to Worry', 'Parchman Farm'
David Bromberg: 'Mr Bojangles'
Ten Years After: 'I Can't Stop From Crying Sometimes'
Procol Harum: 'A Salty Dog'
Leonard Cohen: 'Tonight Will Be Fine'
Jimi Hendrix: 'Power To Love', 'Midnight Lightning', 'Foxy Lady'
Kris Kristofferson: 'Blame It On The Stones', 'The Pilgrim – Chapter 33'
Miles Davis: 'Call It Anythin''

A triple-album set, two LPs of which contain material from the IOW. The inside colour photograph is taken at Afton and features an uncredited shot of the Miles Davis group, filmed from the back of the stage.

Singles

I LUV WIGHT
'Let The World Wash In'/'Medieval Masquerade'
Philips (1970)
The official Festival theme song, issued in a picture sleeve.

GREAT AWAKENING
'Amazing Grace'
London (1969)
The unofficial Festival theme song for both 1969 and 1970, recorded by David Cohen of Country Joe And The Fish.